The Letters of
Paul

with Introduction by

Henry Wansbrough OSB

*All booklets are published thanks to the
generous support of the members of the
Catholic Truth Society*

CATHOLIC TRUTH SOCIETY
PUBLISHERS TO THE HOLY SEE

Contents

❧ INTRODUCTION ❧

THE PAULINE LETTERS

Paul's letters are written to individual communities (and one individual person, Philemon) in response to particular needs and problems which had come to his notice in the Christian communities which he had founded around the mediterranean cities of the Greek-speaking world. With fiery enthusiasm he instructs, encourages, persuades, cajoles, rebukes, lambasts – and in so doing has given Christianity a body of insight, theology and guidance which has formed the backbone of Christian thinking for twenty centuries. Not all Paul's counsels have held their force against the developing values of Christian living – Paul supports the institution of slavery and does not question the brutal Roman regime – but his burning love for Christ and his awareness of the penetration of Christ into every aspect of his followers' life have enriched Christian belief and understanding in a way which no other has achieved.

Paul

Since the letters respond to specific circumstances, a certain knowledge of the communities to which Paul writes, and of Paul's own life and trajectory, helps greatly towards understanding his teaching. A good deal may be gathered about the communities from the letters themselves, supplemented by archaeology and more recent sociological studies. The Acts of the Apostles gives an outline of Paul's activities, though it is inevitably coloured by the author's own interests and concerns. Reservations about this portrait are justified, in that Acts shows no awareness that Paul ever wrote any letters, while Paul himself gives no indication, among all his autobiographical nuggets, that he is a Roman citizen, a status which determines the latter part of the story of Acts. Fascinating nuggets, however, there are, which come together to form a vivid self-portrait of the apostle and pastor, his pride in his origins in Judaism, his dogged endurance of danger and maltreatment, his impassioned rhetoric, his parental (fatherly and motherly) concern for the nurture of his 'children', his parallel yearning to be gone and to be with Christ. Still more important, of course, are his teachings on the human struggle, the saving work of Christ, the indwelling of the Spirit, the community which forms the Body of Christ.

The letters

The letters which have come down to us as Pauline are printed in descending order of length, from longest to shortest, first letters to communities, then letters to individuals. These are not all the letters Paul wrote, for he himself mentions at least one more letter to the Corinthians and one to the Laodiceans. Nor, probably, are they all written personally by Paul, for only seven (Romans, First and Second Corinthians, Galatians, Philippians, First Thessalonians and Philemon) of the thirteen letters are universally accepted as Paul's own writings. Finally, two of the letters are often regarded as composite documents assembled from several shorter notes; this is held to be the origin of Second Corinthians frequently, of Philippians less widely. On authorship of the remaining six letters the Introductions to the individual letters should be consulted.

Dates

Chronologically also there is little agreement; nor would it contribute much to our understanding of the letters if there were. First Thessalonians is usually considered the earliest of Paul's letters, though Galatians is also a serious contender. Central position is conventionally taken by Corinthians and Romans, followed by the 'Captivity Epistles' (*Philippians*, *Philemon*, possibly *Colossians*).

Later still come Ephesians and the Pastoral Epistles. The only two reasonably firm absolute dates are the Damascus Road experience sometime before the death of King Aretas in AD 39/40 (2 *Co* 11:32) and Paul's first visit to Corinth ending with an appearance before the Proconsul Gallio in 51 (*Ac* 18:12). Using the data of Acts, it may be helpful to place Paul's pastoral activity between 37 and 60, but mainly in the 50s.

ᵃ⃝ ROMANS ᵃ⃝

THE LETTER OF PAUL TO THE CHURCH IN ROME

Address

1 ¹From Paul, a servant of Christ Jesus who has been called to be an apostle, and specially chosen to preach the Good News that God ²promised long ago through his prophets in the scriptures.

³This news is about the Son of God who, according to the human nature he took was a descendant of David: ⁴it is about Jesus Christ our Lord who, in the order of the spirit, the spirit of holiness that was in him, was proclaimed Son of God in all his power through his resurrection from the dead. ⁵Through him we received grace and our apostolic mission to preach the obedience of faith to all pagan nations in honour of his name. ⁶You are one of these nations, and by his call belong to Jesus Christ. ⁷To you all, then, who are God's beloved in Rome, called to be saints, may God our Father and the Lord Jesus Christ send grace and peace.

Thanksgiving and prayer

⁸First I thank my God through Jesus Christ for all of you and for the way in which your faith is spoken of all over

the world. ⁹The God I worship spiritually by preaching the Good News of his Son knows that I never fail to mention you in my prayers, ¹⁰and to ask to be allowed at long last the opportunity to visit you, if he so wills. ¹¹For I am longing to see you either to strengthen you by sharing a spiritual gift with you, ¹²or what is better, to find encouragement among you from our common faith. ¹³I want you to know, brothers, that I have often planned to visit you - though until now I have always been prevented - in the hope that I might work as fruitfully among you as I have done among the other pagans. ¹⁴I owe a duty to Greeks[a] just as much as to barbarians, to the educated just as much as to the uneducated, ¹⁵and it is this that makes me want to bring the Good News to you too in Rome.

SALVATION BY FAITH

I. JUSTIFICATION

The theme stated

¹⁶For I am not ashamed of the Good News: it is the power of God saving all who have faith - Jews first, but Greeks as well - ¹⁷since this is what reveals the justice of God to us: it shows how faith leads to faith, or as scripture says: *The upright man finds life through faith.*[b]

[1a.] When contrasted with 'barbarians' (as here), 'Greeks' means the inhabitants of the hellenic world, including the Romans; when contrasted with 'Jews', it means the pagans in general. [1b.] Hab 2:4.

A. GOD'S ANGER AGAINST PAGAN AND JEW

God's anger against the pagans

[18]The anger of God is being revealed from heaven against all the impiety and depravity of men who keep truth imprisoned in their wickedness. [19]For what can be known about God is perfectly plain to them since God himself has made it plain. [20]Ever since God created the world his everlasting power and deity - however invisible - have been there for the mind to see in the things he has made. That is why such people are without excuse: [21]they knew God and yet refused to honour him as God or to thank him; instead, they made nonsense out of logic and their empty minds were darkened. [22]The more they called themselves philosophers, the more stupid they grew, [23]until *they exchanged the glory*[c] of the immortal God for a worthless imitation, *for the image* of mortal man, of birds, of quadrupeds and reptiles. [24]That is why God left them to their filthy enjoyments and the practices with which they dishonour their own bodies, [25]since they have given up divine truth for a lie and have worshipped and served creatures instead of the creator, who is blessed for ever. Amen!

[26]That is why God has abandoned them to degrading passions: why their women have turned from natural intercourse to unnatural practices [27]and why their menfolk

---

[1c.] Ps 106:20.

have given up natural intercourse to be consumed with passion for each other, men doing shameless things with men and getting an appropriate reward for their perversion.

[28]In other words, since they refused to see it was rational to acknowledge God, God has left them to their own irrational ideas and to their monstrous behaviour. [29]And so they are steeped in all sorts of depravity, rottenness, greed and malice, and addicted to envy, murder, wrangling, treachery and spite. [30]Libellers, slanderers, enemies of God, rude, arrogant and boastful; enterprising in sin, rebellious to parents, [32]without brains, honour, love or pity. [33]They know what God's verdict is: that those who behave like this deserve to die - and yet they do it; and what is worse, encourage others to do the same.

The Jews are not exempt from God's anger

2 [1]So no matter who you are, if you pass judgement you have no excuse. In judging others you condemn yourself, since you behave no differently from those you judge. [2]We know that God condemns that sort of behaviour impartially: [3]and when you judge those who behave like this while you are doing exactly the same, do you think you will escape God's judgement? [4]Or are you abusing his abundant goodness, patience and toleration, not realising that this goodness of God is meant to lead you to repentance? [5]Your stubborn refusal to repent is only adding to the anger God will have towards you on that day of

anger when his just judgements will be made known. *⁶He will repay each one as his works deserve.*[a] ⁷For those who sought renown and honour and immortality by always doing good there will be eternal life; ⁸for the unsubmissive who refused to take truth for their guide and took depravity instead, there will be anger and fury. ⁹Pain and suffering will come to every human being who employs himself in evil - Jews first, but Greeks as well; ¹⁰renown, honour and peace will come to everyone who does good - Jews first, but Greeks as well. ¹¹God has no favourites.

The Law will not save them

¹²Sinners who were not subject to the Law will perish all the same, without that Law; sinners who were under the Law will have that Law to judge them. ¹³It is not listening to the Law but keeping it that will make people holy in the sight of God. ¹⁴For instance, pagans who never heard of the Law but are led by reason to do what the Law commands, may not actually 'possess' the Law, but they can be said to 'be' the Law. ¹⁵They can point to the substance of the Law engraved on their hearts - they can call a witness, that is, their own conscience - they have accusation and defence, that is, their own inner mental dialogue.[b] ¹⁶...on the day when, according to the Good News I preach, God, through Jesus Christ, judges the secrets of mankind.

2a. Ps 6:12. 2b. This verse follows on from v.13.

¹⁷If you call yourself a Jew, if you really trust in the Law and are proud of your God, ¹⁸if you know God's will through the Law and can tell what is right, ¹⁹if you are convinced you can guide the blind and be a beacon to those in the dark, ²⁰if you can teach the ignorant and instruct the unlearned because your Law embodies all knowledge and truth, ²¹then why not teach yourself as well as the others? You preach against stealing, yet you steal; ²²you forbid adultery, yet you commit adultery; you despise idols, yet you rob their temples. ²³By boasting about the Law and then disobeying it, you bring God into contempt. ²⁴As scripture says: *It is your fault that the name of God is blasphemed among the pagans.*

Circumcision will not save them

²⁵It is a good thing to be circumcised if you keep the Law; but if you break the Law, you might as well have stayed uncircumcised. ²⁶If a man who is not circumcised obeys the commandments of the Law, surely that makes up for not being circumcised? ²⁷More than that, the man who keeps the Law, even though he has not been physically circumcised, is a living condemnation of the way you disobey the Law in spite of being circumcised and having it all written down. ²⁸To be a Jew is not just to look like a Jew, and circumcision is more than a physical operation. ²⁹The real Jew is the one who is inwardly a Jew, and the real

circumcision is in the heart - something not of the letter but of the spirit. A Jew like that may not be praised by man, but he will be praised by God.

God's promises will not save them

3 [1]Well then, is a Jew any better off? Is there any advantage in being circumcised? [2]A great advantage in every way. First, the Jews are the people to whom God's message was entrusted. [3]What if some of them were unfaithful? Will their lack of fidelity cancel God's fidelity? [4]That would be absurd. God will always be true even though *everyone* proves to be *false*;[a] so scripture says: *In all you say your justice shows, and when you are judged you win your case.*[b] [5]But if our lack of holiness makes God demonstrate his integrity, how can we say God is unjust when - to use a human analogy - he gets angry with us in return? [6]That would be absurd, it would mean God could never judge the world. [7]You might as well say that since my untruthfulness makes God demonstrate his truthfulness and thus gives him glory, I should not be judged to be a sinner at all. [8]That would be the same as saying: Do evil as a means to good. Some slanderers have accused us of teaching this, but they are justly condemned.

[3a.] Ps 116:11. [3b.] Ps 51:4 (LXX).

All are guilty

⁹Well: are we any better off? Not at all: as we said before, Jews and Greeks are all under sin's dominion. ¹⁰As scripture says:

> *There is not a good man left, no, not one:*
> ¹¹*there is not one who understands,*
> *not one who looks for God.*
> ¹²*All have turned aside, tainted all alike;*
> *there is not one good man left, not a single one.*
> ¹³*Their throats are yawning graves;*
> *their tongues are full of deceit.*
> *Vipers' venom is on their lips,*
> ¹⁴*bitter curses fill their mouths.*
> ¹⁵*Their feet are swift when blood is to be shed,*
> ¹⁶*wherever they go there is havoc and ruin.*
> ¹⁷*They know nothing of the way of peace,*
> ¹⁸*there is no fear of God before their eyes.*[c]

¹⁹Now all this that the Law says is said, as we know, for the benefit of those who are subject to the Law, but it is meant to silence everyone and to lay the whole world open to God's judgement; ²⁰and this is because *no one can be justified in the sight of*[d] God by keeping the Law: all that law does is to tell us what is sinful.

3[c]. Quotations from Ps 14, Ps 5, Ps 140, Ps 10, Is 59, Ps 36.   3[d]. Ps 143:2.

B. FAITH AND THE JUSTICE OF GOD

The revelation of God's justice

[21]God's justice that was made known through the Law and the Prophets has now been revealed outside the Law, [22]since it is the same justice of God that comes through faith to everyone, Jew and pagan alike, who believes in Jesus Christ. [23]Both Jew and pagan sinned and forfeited God's glory, [24]and both are justified through the free gift of his grace by being redeemed in Christ Jesus [25]who was appointed by God to sacrifice his life so as to win reconciliation through faith. In this way God makes his justice known; first, for the past, when sins went unpunished because he held his hand, [26]then, for the present age, by showing positively that he is just, and that he justifies everyone who believes in Jesus.

What faith does

[27]So what becomes of our boasts? There is no room for them. What sort of law excludes them? The sort of law that tells us what to do? On the contrary, it is the law of faith, [28]since, as we see it, a man is justified by faith and not by doing something the Law tells him to do. [29]Is God the God of Jews alone and not of the pagans too? Of the pagans too, most certainly, [30]since there is only one God, and he is the one who will justify the circumcised because of their faith and justify the

uncircumcised through their faith. [31]Do we mean that faith makes the Law pointless? Not at all: we are giving the Law its true value.

C. THE EXAMPLE OF ABRAHAM

Abraham justified by faith

4 [1]Apply this to Abraham, the ancestor from whom we are all descended. [2]If Abraham was justified as a reward for doing something, he would really have had something to boast about, though not in God's sight [3]because scripture says: *Abraham put his faith in God, and this faith was considered as justifying him.*[a] [4]If a man has work to show, his wages are not considered as a favour but as his due; [5]but when a man has nothing to show except faith in the one who justifies sinners, then his faith is considered as justifying him. [6]And David says the same: a man is happy if God considers him righteous, irrespective of good deeds:

> [7]*Happy those whose crimes are forgiven,*
> *whose sins are blotted out;*
> [8]*happy the man whom the Lord considers sinless.*[b]

[4a.] Gn 15:6.   [4b.] Ps 32:1-2.

Justified before circumcision

⁹Is this happiness meant only for the circumcised, or is it meant for others as well? Think of Abraham again: *his faith*, we say, *was considered as justifying him,* ¹⁰but when was this done? When he was already circumcised or before he had been circumcised? It was before he had been circumcised, not after; ¹¹and when he was *circumcised* later it was only *as a sign* and guarantee that the faith he had before his circumcision justified him. In this way Abraham became the ancestor of all uncircumcised believers, so that they too might be considered righteous; ¹²and ancestor, also, of those who though circumcised do not rely on that fact alone, but follow our ancestor Abraham along the path of faith he trod before he had been circumcised.

Not justified by obedience to the Law

¹³The promise of inheriting the world was not made to Abraham and his descendants on account of any law but on account of the righteousness which consists in faith. ¹⁴If the world is only to be inherited by those who submit to the Law, then faith is pointless and the promise worth nothing. ¹⁵Law involves the possibility of punishment for breaking the law - only where there is no law can that be avoided. ¹⁶That is why what fulfils the promise depends on faith, so that it may be a free gift and be available to all of Abraham's descendants, not only those who belong

to the Law but also those who belong to the faith of Abraham who is the father of all of us. [17]As scripture says: *I have made you the ancestor of many nations*[c] - Abraham is our father in the eyes of God, in whom he put his faith, and who brings the dead to life and calls into being what does not exist.

Abraham's faith, a model of Christian faith

[18]Though it seemed Abraham's hope could not be fulfilled, he hoped and he believed, and through doing so he did become *the father of many nations* exactly as he had been promised: *Your descendants will be as many as the stars.*[d] [19]Even the thought that his body was past fatherhood - he was about a hundred years old - and Sarah too old to become a mother, did not shake his belief. [20]Since God had promised it, Abraham refused either to deny it or even to doubt it, but drew strength from faith and gave glory to God, [21]convinced that God had power to do what he had promised. [22]This is the faith that was *'considered as justifying him'*. [23]Scripture however does not refer only to him but to us as well when it says that his faith was thus 'considered'; [24]our faith too will be 'considered' if we believe in him who raised Jesus our Lord from the dead, [25]Jesus who was *put to death for our sins*[e] and raised to life to justify us.

---

[c] Gn 17:5 (the same chapter to which allusion is made in v.11, above). [d] Gn 15:5. [e] Is 53:5,6.

II. SALVATION

Faith guarantees salvation

5 [1]So far then we have seen that, through our Lord Jesus Christ, by faith we are judged righteous and at peace with God, [2]since it is by faith and through Jesus that we have entered this state of grace in which we can boast about looking forward to God's glory. [3]But that is not all we can boast about; we can boast about our sufferings. These sufferings bring patience, as we know, [4]and patience brings perseverance, and perseverance brings hope, [5]and this hope is not deceptive, because the love of God has been poured into our hearts by the Holy Spirit which has been given us. [6]We were still helpless when at his appointed moment Christ died for sinful men. [7]It is not easy to die even for a good man - though of course for someone really worthy, a man might be prepared to die - [8]but what proves that God loves us is that Christ died for us while we were still sinners. [9]Having died to make us righteous, is it likely that he would now fail to save us from God's anger? [10]When we were reconciled to God by the death of his Son, we were still enemies; now that we have been reconciled, surely we may count on being saved by the life of his Son? [11]Not merely because we have been reconciled but because we are filled with joyful trust in God, through our Lord Jesus Christ, through whom we have already gained our reconciliation.

A. DELIVERANCE FROM SIN AND DEATH AND LAW

Adam and Jesus Christ

[12]Well then, sin *entered the world* through one man, and through sin death, and thus death has spread through the whole human race because everyone has sinned. [13]Sin existed in the world long before the Law was given. There was no law and so no one could be accused of the sin of 'law-breaking', [14]yet death reigned over all from Adam to Moses, even though their sin, unlike that of Adam, was not a matter of breaking a law.

Adam prefigured the One to come, [15]but the gift itself considerably outweighed the fall. If it is certain that through one man's fall so many died, it is even more certain that divine grace, coming through the one man, Jesus Christ, came to so many as an abundant free gift. [16]The results of the gift also outweigh the results of one man's sin: for after one single fall came judgement with a verdict of condemnation, now after many falls comes grace with its verdict of acquittal. [17]If it is certain that death reigned over everyone as the consequence of one man's fall, it is even more certain that one man, Jesus Christ, will cause everyone to reign in life who receives the free gift that he does not deserve, of being made righteous. [18]Again, as one man's fall brought condemnation on everyone, so the good act of one man brings everyone life and makes them justified. [19]As by one man's disobedience many were made sinners, so by one man's obedience many will be made righteous. ²⁰When law came, it was to multiply the opportunities of failing, but however great the number of sins committed, grace was even greater; ²¹and so, just as sin reigned wherever there was death, so grace will reign to bring eternal life thanks to the righteousness that comes through Jesus Christ our Lord.

Baptism

6 ¹Does it follow that we should remain in sin so as to let grace have greater scope? ²Of course not. We are dead to sin, so how can we continue to live in it? ³You have been taught that when we were baptised in Christ Jesus we were baptised in his death; ⁴in other words, when we were baptised we went into the tomb with him and joined him in death, so that as Christ was raised from the dead by the Father's glory, we too might live a new life.

⁵If in union with Christ we have imitated his death, we shall also imitate him in his resurrection. ⁶We must realise that our former selves have been crucified with him to destroy this sinful body and to free us from the slavery of sin. ⁷When a man dies, of course, he has finished with sin.

⁸But we believe that having died with Christ we shall return to life with him: ⁹Christ, as we know, having been raised from the dead will never die again. Death has no power over him any more. ¹⁰When he died, he died, once for all, to sin, so his life now is life with God; ¹¹and in that

way, you too must consider yourselves to be dead to sin but alive for God in Christ Jesus.

Holiness, not sin, to be the master

[12]That is why you must not let sin reign in your mortal bodies or command your obedience to bodily passions, [13]why you must not let any part of your body turn into an unholy weapon fighting on the side of sin; you should, instead, offer yourselves to God, and consider yourselves dead men brought back to life; you should make every part of your body into a weapon fighting on the side of God; [14]and then sin will no longer dominate your life, since you are living by grace and not by law.

The Christian is freed from the slavery of sin

[15]Does the fact that we are living by grace and not by law mean that we are free to sin? Of course not. [16]You know that if you agree to serve and obey a master you become his slaves. You cannot be slaves of sin that leads to death and at the same time slaves of obedience that leads to righteousness. [17]You were once slaves of sin, but thank God you submitted without reservation to the creed you were taught. [18]You may have been freed from the slavery of sin, but only to become 'slaves' of righteousness. [19]If I may use human terms to help your natural weakness: as once you put your bodies at the

service of vice and immorality, so now you must put them at the service of righteousness for your sanctification.

The reward of sin and the reward of holiness

[20]When you were slaves of sin, you felt no obligation to righteousness, [21]and what did you get from this? Nothing but experiences that now make you blush, since that sort of behaviour ends in death. [22]Now, however, you have been set free from sin, you have been made slaves of God, and you get a reward leading to your sanctification and ending in eternal life. [23]For the wage paid by sin is death; the present given by God is eternal life in Christ Jesus our Lord.

The Christian is not bound by the Law

7 [1]Brothers, those of you who have studied law will know that laws affect a person only during his lifetime. [2]A married woman, for instance, has legal obligations to her husband while he is alive, but all these obligations come to an end if the husband dies. [3]So if she gives herself to another man while her husband is still alive, she is legally an adulteress; but after her husband is dead her legal obligations come to an end, and she can marry someone else without becoming an adulteress. [4]That is why you, my brothers, who through the body of Christ are now dead to the Law, can now give yourselves to another husband, to

him who rose from the dead to make us productive for God. [5]Before our conversion[a] our sinful passions, quite unsubdued by the Law, fertilised our bodies to make them give birth to death. [6]But now we are rid of the Law, freed by death from our imprisonment, free to serve in the new spiritual way and not the old way of a written law.

The function of the Law

[7]Does it follow that the Law itself is sin? Of course not. What I mean is that I should not have known what sin was except for the Law. I should not for instance have known what it means to covet if the Law had not said *You shall not covet.* [8]But it was this commandment that sin took advantage of to produce all kinds of covetousness in me, for when there is no Law, sin is dead.

[9]Once, when there was no Law, I[b] was alive; but when the commandment came, sin came to life [10]and I died: the commandment was meant to lead me to life but it turned out to mean death for me, [11]because sin took advantage of the commandment to mislead me, and so sin, through that commandment, killed me.

[12]The Law is sacred, and what it commands is sacred, just and good. [13]Does that mean that something good killed me? Of course not. But sin, to show itself in its true colours,

---

[7a.] 'While we were in the flesh'. [7b.] Rhetorical figure; Paul speaks in the person of mankind.

used that good thing to kill me; and thus sin, thanks to the commandment, was able to exercise all its sinful power.

The inward struggle

[14]The Law, of course, as we all know, is spiritual; but I am unspiritual; I have been sold as a slave to sin. [15]I cannot understand my own behaviour. I fail to carry out the things I want to do, and I find myself doing the very things I hate. [16]When I act against my own will, that means I have a self that acknowledges that the Law is good, [17]and so the thing behaving in that way is not my self but sin living in me. [18]The fact is, I know of nothing good living in me - living, that is, in my unspiritual self - for though the will to do what is good is in me, the performance is not, [19]with the result that instead of doing the good things I want to do, I carry out the sinful things I do not want. [20]When I act against my will, then, it is not my true self doing it, but sin which lives in me.

[21]In fact, this seems to be the rule, that every single time I want to do good it is something evil that comes to hand. [22]In my inmost self I dearly love God's Law, but [23]I can see that my body follows a different law that battles against the law which my reason dictates. This is what makes me a prisoner of that law of sin which lives inside my body.

[24]What a wretched man I am! Who will rescue me from this body doomed to death? [25]Thanks be to God through Jesus Christ our Lord!

In short, it is I who with my reason serve the Law of God, and no less I who serve in my unspiritual self the law of sin.

B. THE CHRISTIAN'S SPIRITUAL LIFE

The life of the spirit

8 [1]The reason, therefore, why those who are in Christ Jesus are not condemned, [2]is that the law of the spirit of life in Christ Jesus has set you free from the law of sin and death. [3]God has done what the Law, because of our unspiritual nature,[a] was unable to do. God dealt with sin by sending his own Son in a body as physical as any sinful body, and in that body God condemned sin. [4]He did this in order that the Law's just demands might be satisfied in us, who behave not as our unspiritual nature but as the spirit dictates.

[5]The unspiritual are interested only in what is unspiritual, but the spiritual are interested in spiritual things. [6]It is death to limit oneself to what is unspiritual; life and peace can only come with concern for the spiritual. [7]That is because to limit oneself to what is unspiritual is to be at enmity with God: such a limitation never could and never does submit to God's law. [8]People who are interested only in unspiritual things can never be pleasing to God. [9]Your interests, however, are not in the unspiritual, but in

---

[8a.] 'flesh'.

the spiritual, since the Spirit of God has made his home in you. In fact, unless you possessed the Spirit of Christ you would not belong to him. [10]Though your body may be dead it is because of sin, but if Christ is in you then your spirit is life itself because you have been justified; [11]and if the Spirit of him who raised Jesus from the dead is living in you, then he who raised Jesus from the dead will give life to your own mortal bodies through his Spirit living in you.

[12]So then, my brothers, there is no necessity for us to obey our unspiritual selves or to live unspiritual lives. [13]If you do live in that way, you are doomed to die; but if by the Spirit you put an end to the misdeeds of the body you will live.

Children of God

[14]Everyone moved by the Spirit is a son of God. [15]The spirit you received is not the spirit of slaves bringing fear into your lives again; it is the spirit of sons, and it makes us cry out, 'Abba, Father!'[b] [16]The Spirit himself and our spirit bear united witness that we are children of God. [17]And if we are children we are heirs as well: heirs of God and coheirs with Christ, sharing his sufferings so as to share his glory.

Glory as our destiny

[18]I think that what we suffer in this life can never be compared to the glory, as yet unrevealed, which is waiting

---

[8] [b]. The prayer of Christ in Gethsemane.

27

for us. [19]The whole creation is eagerly waiting for God to reveal his sons. [20]It was not for any fault on the part of creation that it was made unable to attain its purpose, it was made so by God; but creation still retains the hope [21]of being freed, like us, from its slavery to decadence, to enjoy the same freedom and glory as the children of God. [22]From the beginning till now the entire creation, as we know, has been groaning in one great act of giving birth; [23]and not only creation, but all of us who possess the first-fruits of the Spirit, we too groan inwardly as we wait for our bodies to be set free. [24]For we must be content to hope that we shall be saved - our salvation is not in sight, we should not have to be hoping for it if it were - [25]but, as I say, we must hope to be saved since we are not saved yet - it is something we must wait for with patience.

[26]The Spirit too comes to help us in our weakness. For when we cannot choose words in order to pray properly, the Spirit himself expresses our plea in a way that could never be put into words, [27]and God who knows everything in our hearts knows perfectly well what he means, and that the pleas of the saints expressed by the Spirit are according to the mind of God.

God has called us to share his glory

[28]We know that by turning everything to their good God co-operates with all those who love him, with all those that he has called according to his purpose. [29]They

are the ones he chose specially long ago and intended to become true images of his Son, so that his Son might be the eldest of many brothers. ³⁰He called those he intended for this; those he called he justified, and with those he justified he shared his glory.

A hymn to God's love

³¹After saying this, what can we add? With God on our side who can be against us? ³²Since God did not spare his own Son, but gave him up to benefit us all, we may be certain, after such a gift, that he will not refuse anything he can give. ³³Could anyone accuse those that God has chosen? When God acquits, ³⁴could anyone condemn? Could Christ Jesus? No! He not only died for us - he rose from the dead, and there at God's right hand he stands and pleads for us.

³⁵Nothing therefore can come between us and the love of Christ, even if we are troubled or worried, or being persecuted, or lacking food or clothes, or being threatened or even attacked. ³⁶As scripture promised: *For your sake we are being massacred daily, and reckoned as sheep for the slaughter.*[c] ³⁷These are the trials through which we triumph, by the power of him who loved us.

³⁸For I am certain of this: neither death nor life, no angel, no prince, nothing that exists, nothing still to come, not any power, ³⁹or height or depth,[d] nor any created thing,

---

8 c. Ps 44:11.   3 d. 'powers', 'heights' and 'depths' are probably cosmic forces hostile to mankind.

can ever come between us and the love of God made visible in Christ Jesus our Lord.

C. THE PLACE OF ISRAEL

The privileges of Israel

9 [1]What I want to say now is no pretence; I say it in union with Christ - it is the truth - my conscience in union with the Holy Spirit assures me of it too. [2]What I want to say is this: my sorrow is so great, my mental anguish so endless, [3]I would willingly be condemned[a] and be cut off from Christ if it could help my brothers of Israel, my own flesh and blood. [4]They were adopted as sons, they were given the glory and the covenants; the Law and the ritual were drawn up for them, and the promises were made to them. [5]They are descended from the patriarchs and from their flesh and blood came Christ who is above all, God for ever blessed! Amen.

God has kept his promise

[6]Does this mean that God has failed to keep his promise? Of course not. Not all those who descend from Israel are Israel; [7]not all the descendants of Abraham are his true children. Remember: *It is through Isaac that your name will be carried on,*[b] [8]which means that it is not

---

[9a] *Anathema*, cursed and excommunicated. [9b] Gn 21:12.

physical descent that decides who are the children of God; it is only the children of the promise who will count as the true descendants. ⁹The actual words in which the promise was made were: *I shall visit you* at such and such a time, *and Sarah will have a son.*ᶜ ¹⁰Even more to the point is what was said to Rebecca when she was pregnant by our ancestor Isaac, ¹¹but before her twin children were born and before either had done good or evil. In order to stress that God's choice is free, ¹²since it depends on the one who calls, not on human merit, Rebecca was told: *the elder shall serve the younger,*ᵈ ¹³or as scripture says elsewhere: *I showed my love for Jacob and my hatred for Esau.*ᵉ

God is not unjust

¹⁴Does it follow that God is unjust? Of course not. ¹⁵Take what God said to Moses: *I have mercy on whom I will, and I show pity to whom I please.*ᶠ ¹⁶In other words, the only thing that counts is not what human beings want or try to do, but the mercy of God. ¹⁷For in scripture he says to Pharaoh: *It was for this I raised you up, to use you as a means of showing my power and to make my name known throughout the world.*ᵍ ¹⁸In other words, when God wants to show mercy he does, and when he wants to harden someone's heart he does so.

---

⁹ᶜ Gn 18:10.   ⁹ᵈ Gn 25:23.   ⁹ᵉ Ml 1:2-3.   ⁹ᶠ Ex 33:19.   ⁹ᵍ Ex 9:16.

[19]You will ask me, 'In that case, how can God ever blame anyone, since no one can oppose his will?' [20]But what right have you, a human being, to cross-examine God? *The pot has no right to say to the potter: Why did you make me this shape?*[h] [21]Surely a potter can do what he likes with the clay? It is surely for him to decide whether he will use a particular lump of clay to make a special pot or an ordinary one?

[22]Or else imagine that although God is ready to show his anger and display his power, yet he patiently puts up with the people who make him angry, however much they deserve to be destroyed. [23]He puts up with them for the sake of those other people, to whom he wants to be merciful, to whom he wants to reveal the richness of his glory, people he had prepared for this glory long ago. [24]Well, we are those people; whether we were Jews or pagans we are the ones he has called.

All has been foretold in the Old Testament

[25]That is exactly what God says in Hosea: *I shall say to a people that was not mine, 'You are my people', and to a nation I never loved, 'I love you'.* [26]*Instead of being told, 'You are no people of mine', they will now be called the sons of the living God.*[i] [27]Referring to Israel Isaiah had this to say: *Though Israel should have many descendants as*

---

[9]h. Is 29:16.   [9]i. Ho 2:25 and 2:1.

there are grains of sand on the seashore, only a remnant will be saved, [28]*for without hesitation or delay the Lord will execute his sentence on the earth.*[j] [29]As Isaiah foretold: *Had the Lord of hosts not left us some descendants we should now be like Sodom, we should be like Gomorrah.*[k]

[30]From this it follows that the pagans who were not looking for righteousness found it all the same, a righteousness that comes of faith, [31]while Israel, looking for a righteousness derived from law failed to do what that law required. [32]Why did they fail? Because they relied on good deeds instead of trusting in faith. In other words, they *stumbled over the stumbling-stone*[l] [33]mentioned in scripture: *See how I lay in Zion a stone to stumble over, a rock to trip men up - only those who believe in him will have no cause for shame.*[m]

Israel fails to see that it is God who makes us holy

10 [1]Brothers, I have the very warmest love for the Jews, and I pray to God for them to be saved. [2]I can swear to their fervour for God, but their zeal is misguided. [3]Failing to recognise the righteousness that comes from God, they try to promote their own idea of it, instead of submitting to the righteousness of God. [4]But now the Law has come to an end with Christ, and everyone who has faith may be justified.

[9j] Is 10:22,23.   [9k] Is 1:9.   [9l] Is 8:14.   [9m] Is 28:16.

The testimony of Moses

⁵When Moses refers to being justified by the Law, he writes: *those who keep the Law will draw life from it.*ᵃ ⁶But the righteousness that comes from faith says this: Do not tell yourself you have to bring Christ down - as in the text: *Who will go up to heaven?*ᵇ ⁷or that you have to bring Christ back from the dead - as in the text: *Who will go down to the underworld?* ⁸On the positive side it says: *The word,* that is the faith we proclaim, *is very near to you, it is on your lips and in your heart.* ⁹If your lips confess that Jesus is Lord and if you believe in your heart that God raised him from the dead, then you will be saved. ¹⁰By believing from the heart you are made righteous; by confessing with your lips you are saved. ¹¹When scripture says: *those who believe in him will have no cause for shame,*ᶜ ¹²it makes no distinction between Jew and Greek: all belong to the same Lord who is rich enough, however many ask his help, ¹³*for everyone who calls on the name of the Lord will be saved.*ᵈ

Israel has no excuse

¹⁴But they will not ask his help unless they believe in him, and they will not believe in him unless they have heard of him, and they will not hear of him unless they

---

¹⁰ᵃ· Lv 18:5.   ¹⁰ᵇ· This quotation, and the two following, are a free rendering of Dt 30:12,14.   ¹⁰ᶜ· Is 28:16.   ¹⁰ᵈ· Jl 3:5.

get a preacher, [15]and they will never have a preacher unless one is sent, but as scripture says: *The footsteps of those who bring good news is a welcome sound.*[e] [16]Not everyone, of course, listens to the Good News. As Isaiah says: *Lord, how many believed what we proclaimed?*[f] [17]So faith comes from what is preached, and what is preached comes from the word of Christ.

[18]Let me put the question: is it possible that they did not hear? Indeed they did; in the words of the psalm, *their voice has gone out through all the earth, and their message to the ends of the world.*[g] [19]A second question: is it possible that Israel did not understand? Moses answered this long ago: *I will make you jealous of people who are not even a nation; I will make you angry with an irreligious people.*[h] [20]Isaiah said more clearly: *I have been found by those who did not seek me, and have revealed myself to those who did not consult me;*[i] [21]and referring to Israel he goes on: *Each day I stretched out my hand to a disobedient and rebellious people.*

The remnant of Israel

11 [1]Let me put a further question then: is it possible that *God has rejected his people?*[a] Of course not. I, an Israelite, descended from Abraham through the tribe of

---

[10e.] Is 52:7.   [10f.] Is 53:1.   [10g.] Ps 19:4.   [10h.] Dt 32:21.   [10i.] Is 65:1,2.
[11a.] Ps 94:14.

Benjamin, ²could never agree that God had rejected his people, the people he chose specially long ago. Do you remember what scripture says of Elijah - how he complained to God about Israel's behaviour? ³*Lord, they have killed your prophets and broken down your altars. I, and I only, remain, and they want to kill me.*[b] ⁴What did God say to that? *I have kept for myself seven thousand men who have not bent the knee to Baal.*[c] ⁵Today the same thing has happened: there is a remnant, chosen by grace. ⁶By grace, you notice, nothing therefore to do with good deeds, or grace would not be grace at all!

⁷What follows? It was not Israel as a whole that found what it was seeking, but only the chosen few. The rest were not allowed to see the truth; ⁸as scripture says: *God has given them a sluggish spirit, unseeing eyes and inattentive ears, and they are still like that today.*[d] ⁹And David says: *May their own table prove a trap for them, a snare and a pitfall - let that be their punishment; ¹⁰may their eyes be struck incurably blind, their backs bend for ever.*[e]

The Jews to be restored in the future

¹¹Let me put another question then: have the Jews fallen for ever, or have they just stumbled? Obviously they have not fallen for ever: their fall, though, has saved the pagans in a way the Jews may now well emulate.

[11b] 1 K 19:10,14.   [11c] 1 K 19:18.   [11d] Is 29:10.   [11e] Ps 69:22f.

[12]Think of the extent to which the world, the pagan world, has benefited from their fall and defection - then think how much more it will benefit from the conversion of them all. [13]Let me tell you pagans[f] this: I have been sent to the pagans as their apostle, and I am proud of being sent, [14]but the purpose of it is to make my own people envious of you, and in this way save some of them. [15]Since their rejection meant the reconciliation of the world, do you know what their admission will mean? Nothing less than a resurrection from the dead!

The Jews are still the chosen people

[16]A whole batch of bread is made holy if the first handful of dough is made holy; all the branches are holy if the root is holy. [17]No doubt some of the branches have been cut off, and, like shoots of wild olive, you have been grafted among the rest to share with them the rich sap provided by the olive tree itself, [18]but still, even if you think yourself superior to the other branches, remember that you do not support the root; it is the root that supports you. [19]You will say, 'Those branches were cut off on purpose to let me be grafted in!' True, [20]they were cut off, but through their unbelief; if you still hold firm, it is only thanks to your faith. Rather than making you proud, that should make you afraid. [21]God did not spare the natural branches,

---

[11] f. Converts from paganism.

and he is not likely to spare you. [22]Do not forget that God can be severe as well as kind: he is severe to those who fell, and he is kind to you, but only for as long as he chooses to be, otherwise you will find yourself cut off too, [23]and the Jews, if they give up their unbelief, grafted back in your place. God is perfectly able to graft them back again; [24]after all, if you were cut from your natural wild olive to be grafted unnaturally on to a cultivated olive, it will be much easier for them, the natural branches, to be grafted back on the tree they came from.

The conversion of the Jews

[25]There is a hidden reason for all this, brothers, of which I do not want you to be ignorant, in case you think you know more than you do. One section of Israel has become blind, but this will last only until the whole pagan world has entered, [26]and then after this the rest of Israel will be saved as well. As scripture says: *The liberator will come from Zion, he will banish godlessness from Jacob.* [27]*And this is the covenant I will make with them when I take their sins away.*[g]

[28]The Jews are enemies of God only with regard to the Good News, and enemies only for your sake; but as the chosen people, they are still loved by God, loved for the sake of their ancestors. [29]God never takes back his gifts or revokes his choice.

---

[11] g. Is 27:9.

[30]Just as you changed from being disobedient to God, and now enjoy mercy because of their disobedience, [31]so those who are disobedient now - and only because of the mercy shown to you - will also enjoy mercy eventually. [32]God has imprisoned all men in their own disobedience only to show mercy to all mankind.

A hymn to God's mercy and wisdom

[33]How rich are the depths of God - how deep his wisdom and knowledge - and how impossible to penetrate his motives or understand his methods! [34]*Who could ever know the mind of the Lord? Who could ever be his counsellor?* [35]*Who could ever give him anything or lend him anything?*[h] [36]All that exists comes from him; all is by him and for him. To him be glory for ever! Amen.

EXHORTATION

Spiritual worship

12 [1]Think of God's mercy, my brothers, and worship him, I beg you, in a way that is worthy of thinking beings, by offering your living bodies as a holy sacrifice, truly pleasing to God. [2]Do not model yourselves on the behaviour of the world around you, but let your behaviour change, modelled by your new mind. This is

---

[11 h.] Is 40:13.

the only way to discover the will of God and know what is good, what it is that God wants, what is the perfect thing to do.

Humility and charity

[3]In the light of the grace I have received I want to urge each one among you not to exaggerate his real importance. Each of you must judge himself soberly by the standard of the faith God has given him. [4]Just as each of our bodies has several parts and each part has a separate function, [5]so all of us, in union with Christ, form one body, and as parts of it we belong to each other. [6]Our gifts differ according to the grace given us. If your gift is prophecy, then use it as your faith suggests; [7]if administration, then use it for administration; if teaching, then use it for teaching. [8]Let the preachers deliver sermons, the almsgivers give freely, the officials be diligent, and those who do works of mercy do them cheerfully.

[9]Do not let your love be a pretence, but sincerely prefer good to evil. [10]Love each other as much as brothers should, and have a profound respect for each other. [11]Work for the Lord with untiring effort and with great earnestness of spirit. [12]If you have hope, this will make you cheerful. Do not give up if trials come; and keep on praying. [13]If any of the saints are in need you must share with them; and you should make hospitality your special care.

Charity to everyone, including enemies

[14]Bless those who persecute you: never curse them, bless them. [15]Rejoice with those who rejoice and be sad with those in sorrow. [16]Treat everyone with equal kindness; never be condescending but make real friends with the poor. Do not allow yourself to become self-satisfied. [17]Never repay evil with evil but let everyone see that you are interested only in the highest ideals. [18]Do all you can to live at peace with everyone. [19]Never try to get revenge; leave that, my friends, to God's anger. As scripture says: *vengeance is mine - I will pay them back,*[a] the Lord promises. [20]But there is more: *If your enemy is hungry, you should give him food, and if he is thirsty, let him drink. Thus you heap red-hot coals on his head.*[b] [21]Resist evil and conquer it with good.

Submission to civil authority

13 [1]You must all obey the governing authorities. Since all government comes from God, the civil authorities were appointed by God, [2]and so anyone who resists authority is rebelling against God's decision, and such an act is bound to be punished. [3]Good behaviour is not afraid of magistrates; only criminals have anything to fear. If you want to live without being afraid of authority, you must live honestly and authority may even honour you. [4]The state is

---

[12 a.] Dt 32:35. [12 b.] Pr 25:21-22.

there to serve God for your benefit. If you break the law, however, you may well have fear: the bearing of the sword has its significance. The authorities are there to serve God: they carry out God's revenge by punishing wrongdoers. [5]You must obey, therefore, not only because you are afraid of being punished, but also for conscience' sake. [6]This is also the reason why you must pay taxes, since all government officials are God's officers. They serve God by collecting taxes. [7]Pay every government official what he has a right to ask - whether it be direct tax or indirect, fear or honour.

Love and law

[8]Avoid getting into debt, except the debt of mutual love. If you love your fellow men you have carried out your obligations. [9]All the commandments: *You shall not commit adultery, you shall not kill, you shall not steal, you shall not covet,*[a] and so on, are summed up in this single command: *You must love your neighbour as yourself*[b] [10]Love is the one thing that cannot hurt your neighbour; that is why it is the answer to every one of the commandments.

Children of the light

[11]Besides, you know 'the time' has come: you must wake up now: our salvation is even nearer than it was when we were converted. [12]The night is almost over, it

---

[13a.] From the Commandments in Ex 20 and Dt 17.   [13b.] Lv 19:18.

will be daylight soon - let us give up all the things we prefer to do under cover of the dark; let us arm ourselves and appear in the light. [13]Let us live decently as people do in the daytime: no drunken orgies, no promiscuity or licentiousness, and no wrangling or jealousy. [14]Let your armour be the Lord Jesus Christ; forget about satisfying your bodies with all their cravings.

Charity towards the scrupulous

14 [1]If a person's faith is not strong enough, welcome him all the same without starting an argument. [2]People range from those who believe they may eat any sort of meat to those whose faith is so weak they dare not eat anything except vegetables. [3]Meat-eaters must not despise the scrupulous. On the other hand, the scrupulous must not condemn those who feel free to eat anything they choose, since God has welcomed them. [4]It is not for you to condemn someone else's servant: whether he stands or falls it is his own master's business; he will stand, you may be sure, because the Lord has power to make him stand. [5]If one man keeps certain days as holier than others, and another considers all days to be equally holy, each must be left free to hold his own opinion. [6]The one who observes special days does so in honour of the Lord. The one who eats meat also does so in honour of the Lord, since he gives thanks to God; but then the man who abstains does that too in honour of the Lord, and so he also gives God thanks. [7]The life and death of each of us has its influence on others; [8]if we live, we live for the Lord; and if we die, we die for the Lord, so that alive or dead we belong to the Lord. [9]This explains why Christ both died and came to life, it was so that he might be Lord both of the dead and of the living. [10]This is also why you should never pass judgement on a brother or treat him with contempt, as some of you have done. We shall all have to stand before the judgement seat of God; [11]as scripture says: *By my life - it is the Lord who speaks - every knee shall bend before me, and every tongue shall praise God.*[a] [12]It is to God, therefore, that each of us must give an account of himself.

[13]Far from passing judgement on each other, therefore, you should make up your mind never to be the cause of your brother tripping or falling. [14]Now I am perfectly well aware, of course, and I speak for the Lord Jesus, that no food is unclean in itself; however, if someone thinks that a particular food is unclean, then it is unclean for him. [15]And indeed if your attitude to food is upsetting your brother, then you are hardly being guided by charity. You are certainly not free to eat what you like if that means the downfall of someone for whom Christ died.

[14a] Is 45:23.

[16]In short, you must not compromise your privilege, [17]because the kingdom of God does not mean eating or drinking this or that, it means righteousness and peace and joy brought by the Holy Spirit. [18]If you serve Christ in this way you will please God and be respected by men. [19]So let us adopt any custom that leads to peace and our mutual improvement; [20]do not wreck God's work over a question of food. Of course all food is clean, but it becomes evil if by eating it you make somebody else fall away. [21]In such cases the best course is to abstain from meat and wine and anything else that would make your brother trip or fall or weaken in any way.

[22]Hold on to your own belief, as between yourself and God-and consider the man fortunate who can make his decision without going against his conscience. [23]But anybody who eats in a state of doubt is condemned, because he is not in good faith; and every act done in bad faith is a sin.

15 [1]We who are strong have a duty to put up with the qualms of the weak without thinking of ourselves. [2]Each of us should think of his neighbours and help them to become stronger Christians. [3]Christ did not think of himself: the words of scripture - *the insults of those who insult you fall on me*[a] - apply to him. [4]And indeed everything that was written long ago in the scriptures was

---

15 a. Ps 69:9.

meant to teach us something about hope from the examples scripture gives of how people who did not give up were helped by God. ⁵And may he who helps us when we refuse to give up, help you all to be tolerant with each other, following the example of Christ Jesus, ⁶so that united in mind and voice you may give glory to the God and Father of our Lord Jesus Christ.

An appeal for unity

⁷It can only be to God's glory, then, for you to treat each other in the same friendly way as Christ treated you. ⁸The reason Christ became the servant of circumcised Jews was not only so that God could faithfully carry out the promises made to the patriarchs, ⁹it was also to get the pagans to give glory to God for his mercy, as scripture says in one place: *For this I shall praise you among the pagans and sing to your name.*ᵇ ¹⁰And in another place: *Rejoice, pagans, with his people,*ᶜ ¹¹and in a third place: *Let all the pagans praise the Lord, let all the peoples sing his praises.*ᵈ ¹²Isaiah too has this to say: *The root of Jesse will appear, rising up to rule the pagans, and in him the pagans will put their hope.*ᵉ

¹³May the God of hope bring you such joy and peace in your faith that the power of the Holy Spirit will remove all bounds to hope.

---

¹⁵ᵇ Ps 18:50. ¹⁵ᶜ Dt 32:43 (LXX). ¹⁵ᵈ Ps 117:1. ¹⁵ᵉ Is 11:10; 11:1.

EPILOGUE

Paul's ministry

[14]It is not because I have any doubts about you, my brothers; on the contrary I am quite certain that you are full of good intentions, perfectly well instructed and able to advise each other. [15]The reason why I have written to you, and put some things rather strongly, is to refresh your memories, since God has given me this special position. [16]He has appointed me as a priest of Jesus Christ, and I am to carry out my priestly duty by bringing the Good News from God to the pagans, and so make them acceptable as an offering, made holy by the Holy Spirit.

[17]I think I have some reason to be proud of what I, in union with Christ Jesus, have been able to do for God. [18]What I am presuming to speak of, of course, is only what Christ himself has done to win the allegiance of the pagans, using what I have said and done [19]by the power of signs and wonders, by the power of the Holy Spirit. Thus all the way along, from Jerusalem to Illyricum,[f] I have preached Christ's Good News to the utmost of my capacity. [20]I have always, however, made it an unbroken rule never to preach where Christ's name has already been heard. The reason for that was that I had no wish to build on other men's foundations; [21]on the contrary, my

---

[15 f.] The two extremes of Paul's missionary journeys.

chief concern has been to fulfil the text: *Those who have never been told about him will see him, and those who have never heard about him will understand.*[g]

Paul's plans

[22]That is the reason why I have been kept from visiting you so long, [23]though for many years I have been longing to pay you a visit. Now, however, having no more work to do here, [24]I hope to see you on my way to Spain and, after enjoying a little of your company, to complete the rest of the journey with your good wishes. [25]First, however, I must take a present of money to the saints in Jerusalem, [26]since Macedonia and Achaia have decided to send a generous contribution to the poor among the saints at Jerusalem. [27]A generous contribution as it should be, since it is really repaying a debt: the pagans who share the spiritual possessions of these poor people have a duty to help them with temporal possessions. [28]So when I have done this and officially handed over what has been raised, I shall set out for Spain and visit you on the way. [29]I know that when I reach you I shall arrive with rich blessings from Christ.

[30]But I beg you, brothers, by our Lord Jesus Christ and the love of the Spirit, to help me through my dangers by praying to God for me. [31]Pray that I may escape the

---

15 g. Is 52:15.

unbelievers in Judaea, and that the aid I carry to Jerusalem may be accepted by the saints. [32]Then, if God wills, I shall be feeling very happy when I come to enjoy a period of rest among you. [33]May the God of peace be with you all! Amen.

Greetings and good wishes

16 [1]I commend to you our sister Phoebe,[a] a deaconess of the church at Cenchreae. [2]Give her, in union with the Lord, a welcome worthy of saints, and help her with anything she needs: she has looked after a great many people, myself included.

[3]My greetings to Prisca and Aquila, my fellow workers in Christ Jesus, [4]who risked death to save my life:[b] I am not the only one to owe them a debt of gratitude, all the churches among the pagans do as well. [5]My greetings also to the church that meets at their house.

[6]Greetings to my friend Epaenetus, the first of Asia's gifts to Christ; greetings to Mary who worked so hard for you; [7]to those outstanding apostles Andronicus and Junias, my compatriots and fellow prisoners who became Christians before me; [8]to Ampliatus, my friend in the Lord; [9]to Urban, my fellow worker in Christ; to my friend Stachys; [10]to Apelles who has gone through so much for

---

[16 a.] Probably the bearer of the letter.   [16 b.] Probably in Ephesus, either at the time of the riot described in Ac 19 or during Paul's imprisonment there.

Christ; to everyone who belongs to the household of Aristobulus; ¹¹to my compatriot Herodion; to those in the household of Narcissus who belong to the Lord; ¹²to Tryphaena and Tryphosa, who work hard for the Lord; to my friend Persis who has done so much for the Lord; ¹³to Rufus, a chosen servant of the Lord, and to his mother who has been a mother to me too. ¹⁴Greetings to Asyncritus, Phlegon, Hermes, Patrobas, Hermas, and all the brothers who are with them; ¹⁵to Philologus and Julia, Nereus and his sister, and Olympas and all the saints who are with them. ¹⁶Greet each other with a holy kiss. All the churches of Christ send greetings.

A warning and first postscript

¹⁷I implore you, brothers, be on your guard against anybody who encourages trouble or puts difficulties in the way of the doctrine you have been taught. Avoid them. ¹⁸People like that are not slaves of Jesus Christ, they are slaves of their own appetites, confusing the simple-minded with their pious and persuasive arguments. ¹⁹Your fidelity to Christ, anyway, is famous everywhere, and that makes me very happy about you. I only hope that you are also wise in what is good, and innocent of what is bad. ²⁰The God of peace will soon crush Satan beneath your feet. The grace of our Lord Jesus Christ be with you.

Last greetings and second postscript

²¹Timothy, who is working with me, sends his greetings; so do my compatriots, Jason and Sosipater. ²²I, Tertius, who wrote out this letter, greet you in the Lord. ²³Greetings from Gaius, who is entertaining me and from the whole church that meets in his house. Erastus, the city treasurer, sends his greetings; so does our brother Quartus.

Doxology

²⁵Glory to him who is able to give you the strength to live according to the Good News I preach, and in which I proclaim Jesus Christ, the revelation of a mystery kept secret for endless ages, ²⁶but now so clear that it must be broadcast to pagans everywhere to bring them to the obedience of faith. This is only what scripture has predicted, and it is all part of the way the eternal God wants things to be. ²⁷He alone is wisdom; give glory therefore to him through Jesus Christ for ever and ever. Amen.

⚜ 1 CORINTHIANS ⚜

THE FIRST LETTER OF PAUL TO THE CHURCH AT CORINTH

INTRODUCTION

Address and greetings. Thanksgiving

1 ¹I, Paul, appointed by God to be an apostle, together with brother Sosthenes, send greetings ²to the church of God in Corinth, to the holy people of Jesus Christ, who are called to take their place among all the saints everywhere who pray to our Lord Jesus Christ; for he is their Lord no less than ours. ³May God our Father and the Lord Jesus Christ send you grace and peace.

⁴I never stop thanking God for all the graces you have received through Jesus Christ. ⁵I thank him that you have been enriched in so many ways, especially in your teachers and preachers; ⁶the witness to Christ has indeed been strong among you ⁷so that you will not be without any of the gifts of the Spirit while you are waiting for our Lord Jesus Christ to be revealed; ⁸and he will keep you steady and without blame until the last

day, the day of our Lord Jesus Christ, [9]because God by calling you has joined you to his Son, Jesus Christ; and God is faithful.

I. DIVISIONS AND SCANDALS

A. FACTIONS IN THE CORINTHIAN CHURCH

Dissensions among the faithful

[10]All the same, I do appeal to you, brothers, for the sake of our Lord Jesus Christ, to make up the differences between you, and instead of disagreeing among yourselves, to be united again in your belief and practice. [11]From what Chloe's people have been telling me, my dear brothers, it is clear that there are serious differences among you. [12]What I mean are all these slogans that you have, like: 'I am for Paul', 'I am for Apollos', 'I am for Cephas',[a] 'I am for Christ'. [13]Has Christ been parcelled out? Was it Paul that was crucified for you? Were you baptised in the name of Paul? [14]I am thankful that I never baptised any of you after Crispus and Gaius [15]so none of you can say he was baptised in my name. [16]Then there was the family of Stephanas, of course, that I baptised too, but no one else as far as I can remember.

[1a.] Peter.

The true wisdom and the false

[17]For Christ did not send me to baptise, but to preach the Good News, and not to preach that in the terms of philosophy[b] in which the crucifixion of Christ cannot be expressed. [18]The language of the cross may be illogical to those who are not on the way to salvation, but those of us who are on the way see it as God's power to save. [19]As scripture says: *I shall destroy the wisdom of the wise and bring to nothing all the learning of the learned. [20]Where are the philosophers now? Where are the scribes?*[c] Where are any of our thinkers today? Do you see now how God has shown up the foolishness of human wisdom? [21]If it was God's wisdom that human wisdom should not know God, it was because God wanted to save those who have faith through the foolishness of the message that we preach. [22]And so, while the Jews demand miracles and the Greeks look for wisdom, [23]here are we preaching a crucified Christ; to the Jews an obstacle that they cannot get over, to the pagans madness, [24]but to those who have been called, whether they are Jews or Greeks, a Christ who is the power and the wisdom of God. [25]For God's foolishness is wiser than human wisdom, and God's weakness is stronger than human strength.

[1 b] 'wisdom', the term used by Paul for the human wisdom of philosophy and rhetoric. [1 c] Quotations from Is 29:14, Ps 33:10 and Is 33:18 (LXX).

²⁶Take yourselves for instance, brothers, at the time when you were called: how many of you were wise in the ordinary sense of the word, how many were influential people, or came from noble families? ²⁷No, it was to shame the wise that God chose what is foolish by human reckoning, and to shame what is strong that he chose what is weak by human reckoning; ²⁸those whom the world thinks common and contemptible are the ones that God has chosen - those who are nothing at all to show up those who are everything. ²⁹The human race has nothing to boast about to God, ³⁰but you God has made members of Christ Jesus and by God's doing he has become our wisdom, and our virtue, and our holiness, and our freedom. ³¹As scripture says: *if anyone wants to boast, let him boast about the Lord.*[d]

2 ¹As for me, brothers, when I came to you, it was not with any show of oratory or philosophy, but simply to tell you what God had guaranteed. ²During my stay with you, the only knowledge I claimed to have was about Jesus, and only about him as the crucified Christ. ³Far from relying on any power of my own, I came among you in great 'fear and trembling'[a] ⁴and in my speeches and the sermons that I gave, there were none of the arguments that

---

[1d.] Jr 9:22-23.

[2a.] A scriptural cliché frequently used by Paul.

belong to philosophy; only a demonstration of the power
of the Spirit. ⁵And I did this so that your faith should not
depend on human philosophy but on the power of God.

⁶But still we have a wisdom to offer those who have
reached maturity: not a philosophy of our age, it is true,
still less of the masters of our age, which are coming to
their end. ⁷The hidden wisdom of God which we teach in
our mysteries is the wisdom that God predestined to be
for our glory before the ages began. ⁸It is a wisdom that
none of the masters of this age have ever known, or they
would not have crucified the Lord of Glory; ⁹we teach
what scripture calls: *the things that no eye has seen and
no ear has heard, things beyond the mind of man, all that
God has prepared for those who love him.*[b]

¹⁰These are the very things that God has revealed to us
through the Spirit, for the Spirit reaches the depths of
everything, even the depths of God. ¹¹After all, the depths
of a man can only be known by his own spirit, not by any
other man, and in the same way the depths of God can
only be known by the Spirit of God. ¹²Now instead of the
spirit of the world, we have received the Spirit that comes
from God, to teach us to understand the gifts that he has
given us. ¹³Therefore we teach, not in the way in which
philosophy is taught, but in the way that the Spirit teaches
us: we teach spiritual things spiritually. ¹⁴An unspiritual

[2 b.] A free combination of Is 64:3 and Jr 3:16.

person is one who does not accept anything of the Spirit of God: he sees it all as nonsense; it is beyond his understanding because it can only be understood by means of the Spirit. [15]A spiritual man, on the other hand, is able to judge the value of everything, and his own value is not to be judged by other men.[16] As scripture says: *Who can know the mind of the Lord, so who can teach him?*[c] But we are those who have the mind of Christ.

3 [1]Brothers, I myself was unable to speak to you as people of the Spirit: I treated you as sensual men, still infants in Christ. [2]What I fed you with was milk, not solid food, for you were not ready for it; and indeed, you are still not ready for it [3]since you are still unspiritual. Isn't that obvious from all the jealousy and wrangling that there is among you, from the way that you go on behaving like ordinary people? [4]What could be more unspiritual than your slogans, 'I am for Paul' and 'I am for Apollos'?

The place of the Christian preacher

[5]After all, what is Apollos and what is Paul? They are servants who brought the faith to you. Even the different ways in which they brought it were assigned to them by the Lord. [6]I did the planting, Apollos did the watering, but God made things grow. [7]Neither the planter nor the waterer matters: only God, who makes things grow. [8]It is

---

[c] Is 40:13.

all one who does the planting and who does the watering, and each will duly be paid according to his share in the work. [9]We are fellow workers with God; you are God's farm, God's building.

[10]By the grace God gave me, I succeeded as an architect and laid the foundations, on which someone else is doing the building. Everyone doing the building must work carefully. [11]For the foundation, nobody can lay any other than the one which has already been laid, that is Jesus Christ. [12]On this foundation you can build in gold, silver and jewels, or in wood, grass and straw, [13]but whatever the material, the work of each builder is going to be clearly revealed when the day comes. That day will begin with fire, and the fire will test the quality of each man's work. [14]If his structure stands up to it, he will get his wages; [15]if it is burnt down, he will be the loser, and though he is saved himself, it will be as one who has gone through fire.

[16]Didn't you realise that you were God's temple and that the Spirit of God was living among you? [17]If anybody should destroy the temple of God, God will destroy him, because the temple of God is sacred; and you are that temple.

Conclusions

[18]Make no mistake about it: if any one of you thinks of himself as wise, in the ordinary sense of the word, then he must learn to be a fool before he really can be wise.

¹⁹Why? Because the wisdom of this world is foolishness to God. As scripture says: *The Lord knows wise men's thoughts: he knows how useless they are:*[a] ²⁰or again: *God is not convinced by the arguments of the wise*[b] ²¹So there is nothing to boast about in anything human: ²²Paul, Apollos, Cephas, the world, life and death, the present and the future, are all your servants; ²³but you belong to Christ and Christ belongs to God.

4 ¹People must think of us as Christ's servants, stewards entrusted with the mysteries of God. ²What is expected of stewards is that each one should be found worthy of his trust. ³Not that it makes the slightest difference to me whether you, or indeed any human tribunal, find me worthy or not. I will not even pass judgement on myself. ⁴True, my conscience does not reproach me at all, but that does not prove that I am acquitted: the Lord alone is my judge. ⁵There must be no passing of premature judgement. Leave that until the Lord comes; he will light up all that is hidden in the dark and reveal the secret intentions of men's hearts. Then will be the time for each one to have whatever praise he deserves, from God.

⁶Now in everything I have said here, brothers, I have taken Apollos and myself as an example (remember the maxim: 'Keep to what is written'); it is not for you, so

---

3 a. Jb 5:13.   3 b. Ps 94:11.

full of your own importance, to go taking sides for one man against another. ⁷In any case, brother, has anybody given you some special right? What do you have that was not given to you? And if it was given, how can you boast as though it were not? ⁸Is it that you have everything you want - that you are rich already, in possession of your kingdom, with us left outside? Indeed I wish you were really kings, and we could be kings with you! ⁹But instead, it seems to me, God has put us apostles at the end of his parade, with the men sentenced to death; it is true - we have been put on show in front of the whole universe, angels as well as men. ¹⁰Here we are, fools for the sake of Christ, while you are the learned men in Christ; we have no power, but you are influential; you are celebrities, we are nobodies. ¹¹To this day, we go without food and drink and clothes; we are beaten and have no homes; ¹²we work for our living with our own hands. When we are cursed, we answer with a blessing; when we are hounded, we put up with it; ¹³we are insulted and we answer politely. We are treated as the offal of the world, still to this day, the scum of the earth.

An appeal

¹⁴I am saying all this not just to make you ashamed but to bring you, as my dearest children, to your senses. ¹⁵You might have thousands of guardians in Christ, but not more than one father and it was I who begot you in Christ Jesus

by preaching the Good News. [16]That is why I beg you to copy me [17]and why I have sent you Timothy, my dear and faithful son in the Lord: he will remind you of the way that I live in Christ, as I teach it everywhere in all the churches.

[18]When it seemed that I was not coming to visit you, some of you became self-important, [19]but I will be visiting you soon, the Lord willing, and then I shall want to know not what these self-important people have to say, but what they can do, [20]since the kingdom of God is not just words, it is power. [21]It is for you to decide: do I come with a stick in my hand or in a spirit of love and goodwill?

B. INCEST IN CORINTH

5 [1]I have been told as an undoubted fact that one of you is living with his father's wife.[a] This is a case of sexual immorality among you that must be unparalleled even among pagans. [2]How can you be so proud of yourselves? You should be in mourning. A man who does a thing like that ought to have been expelled from the community. [3]Though I am far away in body, I am with you in spirit, and have already condemned the man who did this thing as if I were actually present. [4]When you are assembled together in the name of the Lord Jesus, and I am spiritually present with you, then with the power of

---

[5a.] Stepmother. Lv 18:8 forbids sexual relations with 'your father's wife'.

our Lord Jesus [5]he is to be handed over to Satan so that his sensual body may be destroyed and his spirit saved on the day of the Lord.

[6]The pride that you take in yourselves is hardly to your credit. You must know how even a small amount of yeast is enough to leaven all the dough, [7]so get rid of all the old yeast, and make yourselves into a completely new batch of bread, unleavened as you are meant to be. Christ, our passover, has been sacrificed; [8]let us celebrate the feast, then, by getting rid of all the old yeast of evil and wickedness, having only the unleavened bread of sincerity and truth.[b]

[9]When I wrote in my letter to you not to associate with people living immoral lives, [10]I was not meaning to include all the people in the world who are sexually immoral, any more than I meant to include all usurers and swindlers or idol worshippers. To do that, you would have to withdraw from the world altogether. [11]What I wrote was that you should not associate with a brother Christian who is leading an immoral life, or is a usurer, or idolatrous, or a slanderer, or a drunkard, or is dishonest; you should not even eat a meal with people like that. [12]It is not my business to pass judgement on those outside. Of those who are inside, you can surely be the judges. [13]But of those who are outside, God is the judge.

You must drive out this evil-doer from among you.[c]

[5b] See note a to Jn 19, on the Passover practice.   [5c] Dt 13:6.

C. RECOURSE TO THE PAGAN COURTS

6 [1]How dare one of your members take up a complaint against another in the lawcourts of the unjust[a] instead of before the saints? [2]As you know, it is the saints who are to 'judge the world'; and if the world is to be judged by you, how can you be unfit to judge trifling cases? [3]Since we are also to judge angels, it follows that we can judge matters of everyday life; [4]but when you have had cases of that kind, the people you appointed to try them were not even respected in the Church. [5]You should be ashamed: is there really not one reliable man among you to settle differences between brothers [6]and so one brother brings a court case against another in front of unbelievers? [7]It is bad enough for you to have lawsuits at all against one another: oughtn't you to let yourselves be wronged, and let yourselves be cheated? [8]But you are doing the wronging and the cheating, and to your own brothers.

[9]You know perfectly well that people who do wrong will not inherit the kingdom of God: people of immoral lives, idolaters, adulterers, catamites, sodomites, [10]thieves, usurers, drunkards, slanderers and swindlers will never inherit the kingdom of God. [11]These are the sort of people some of you were once, but now you have

---

[6a.] The pagan magistrates of Corinth.

been washed clean, and sanctified, and justified through the name of the Lord Jesus Christ and through the Spirit of our God.

D. FORNICATION

[12]'For me there are no forbidden things';[b] maybe, but not everything does good. I agree there are no forbidden things for me, but I am not going to let anything dominate me. [13]Food is only meant for the stomach, and the stomach for food; yes, and God is going to do away with both of them. But the body - this is not meant for fornication; it is for the Lord, and the Lord for the body. [14]God, who raised the Lord from the dead, will by his power raise us up too.

[15]You know, surely, that your bodies are members making up the body of Christ; do you think I can take parts of Christ's body and join them to the body of a prostitute? Never! [16]As you know, a man who goes with a prostitute is one body with her, since *the two*, as it is said, *become one flesh*. [17]But anyone who is joined to the Lord is one spirit with him.

---

[b] Probably one of Paul's own sayings which has been misapplied by false teachers: this section of the letter is directed against the libertines, who had been teaching that sexual intercourse was as necessary for the body as food and drink.

[18]Keep away from fornication. All the other sins are committed outside the body; but to fornicate is to sin against your own body. [19]Your body, you know, is the temple of the Holy Spirit, who is in you since you received him from God. You are not your own property; [20]you have been bought and paid for. That is why you should use your body for the glory of God.

II. ANSWERS TO VARIOUS QUESTIONS

A. MARRIAGE AND VIRGINITY

7 [1]Now for the questions about which you wrote. Yes, it is a good thing for a man not to touch a woman; [2]but since sex is always a danger, let each man have his own wife and each woman her own husband. [3]The husband must give his wife what she has the right to expect, and so too the wife to the husband. [4]The wife has no rights over her own body; it is the husband who has them. In the same way, the husband has no rights over his body; the wife has them. [5]Do not refuse each other except by mutual consent, and then only for an agreed time, to leave yourselves free for prayer; then come together again in case Satan should take advantage of your weakness to tempt you. [6]This is a suggestion, not a rule: [7]I should like everyone to be like me, but everybody has his own particular gifts from God, one with a gift for one thing and another with a gift for the opposite.

⁸There is something I want to add for the sake of widows and those who are not married: it is a good thing for them to stay as they are, like me, ⁹but if they cannot control the sexual urges, they should get married, since it is better to be married than to be tortured.

¹⁰For the married I have something to say, and this is not from me but from the Lord: a wife must not leave her husband - ¹¹or if she does leave him, she must either remain unmarried or else make it up with her husband - nor must a husband send his wife away.

¹²The rest is from me and not from the Lord. If a brother has a wife who is an unbeliever, and she is content to live with him, he must not send her away; ¹³and if a woman has an unbeliever for her husband, and he is content to live with her, she must not leave him. ¹⁴This is because the unbelieving husband is made one with the saints through his wife, and the unbelieving wife is made one with the saints through her husband. If this were not so, your children would be unclean, whereas in fact they are holy. ¹⁵However, if the unbelieving partner does not consent, they may separate; in these circumstances, the brother or sister is not tied: God has called you to a life of peace. ¹⁶If you are a wife, it may be your part to save your husband, for all you know; if a husband, for all you know, it may be your part to save your wife.

[17]For the rest, what each one has is what the Lord has given him and he should continue as he was when God's call reached him. This is the ruling that I give in all the churches. [18]If anyone had already been circumcised at the time of his call, he need not disguise it, and anyone who was uncircumcised at the time of his call need not be circumcised; [19]because to be circumcised or uncircumcised means nothing: what does matter is to keep the commandments of God. [20]Let everyone stay as he was at the time of his call. [21]If, when you were called, you were a slave, do not let this bother you; but if you should have the chance of being free, accept it. [22]A slave, when he is called in the Lord, becomes the Lord's freedman, and a freeman called in the Lord becomes Christ's slave. [23]You have all been bought and paid for; do not be slaves of other men. [24]Each one of you, my brothers, should stay as he was before God at the time of his call.

[25]About remaining celibate, I have no directions from the Lord but give my own opinion as one who, by the Lord's mercy, has stayed faithful. [26]Well then, I believe that in these present times of stress this is right: that it is good for a man to stay as he is. [27]If you are tied to a wife, do not look for freedom; if you are free of a wife, then do not look for one. [28]But if you marry, it is no sin, and it is not a sin for a young girl to get married. They will have their troubles, though, in their married life, and I should like to spare you that.

[29]Brothers, this is what I mean: our time is growing short. Those who have wives should live as though they had none, [30]and those who mourn should live as though they had nothing to mourn for; those who are enjoying life should live as though there were nothing to laugh about; those whose life is buying things should live as though they had nothing of their own; [31]and those who have to deal with the world should not become engrossed in it. I say this because the world as we know it is passing away.

[32]I would like to see you free from all worry. An unmarried man can devote himself to the Lord's affairs, all he need worry about is pleasing the Lord; [33]but a married man has to bother about the world's affairs and devote himself to pleasing his wife: [34]he is torn two ways. In the same way an unmarried woman, like a young girl, can devote herself to the Lord's affairs; all she need worry about is being holy in body and spirit. The married woman, on the other hand, has to worry about the world's affairs and devote herself to pleasing her husband. [35]I say this only to help you, not to put a halter round your necks, but simply to make sure that everything is as it should be, and that you give your undivided attention to the Lord.

[36]Still, if there is anyone who feels that it would not be fair to his daughter to let her grow too old for marriage, and that he should do something about it, he is free to do as he likes: he is not sinning if there is a marriage. [37]On the other hand, if someone has firmly made his mind up, without any

compulsion and in complete freedom of choice, to keep his daughter as she is, he will be doing a good thing. [38]In other words, the man who sees that his daughter is married has done a good thing but the man who keeps his daughter unmarried has done something even better.[a]

[39]A wife is tied as long as her husband is alive. But if the husband dies, she is free to marry anybody she likes, only it must be in the Lord. [40]She would be happier, in my opinion, if she stayed as she is - and I too have the Spirit of God, I think.

B. FOOD OFFERED TO IDOLS

General principles

8 [1]Now about food sacrificed to idols. 'We all have knowledge'; yes, that is so, but knowledge gives self-importance - it is love that makes the building grow. [2]A man may imagine he understands something, but still not understand anything in the way that he ought to. [3]But any man who loves God is known by him. [4]Well then, about eating food sacrificed to idols:[a] we know that idols do not

---

[7a.] 'daughter' is not the only possible word; this passage has been read as alluding to the practice of a man and a woman living together under vows of chastity; a practice for which there is evidence of a later date.

[8a.] At feasts and public ceremonies, portions of the food were 'sacrificed' and went to the gods, the priests and the donors; the whole of the food was regarded as dedicated, whether it was eaten at a ceremonial meal or part of it sold in the markets.

really exist in the world and that there is no god but the One. ⁵And even if there were things called gods, either in the sky or on earth - where there certainly seem to be 'gods' and 'lords' in plenty - ⁶still for us there is one God, the Father, from whom all things come and for whom we exist; and there is one Lord, Jesus Christ, through whom all things come and through whom we exist.

The claims of love

⁷Some people, however, do not have this knowledge. There are some who have been so long used to idols that they eat this food as though it really had been sacrificed to the idol, and their conscience, being weak, is defiled by it. ⁸Food, of course, cannot bring us in touch with God: we lose nothing if we refuse to eat, we gain nothing if we eat. ⁹Only be careful that you do not make use of this freedom in a way that proves a pitfall for the weak. ¹⁰Suppose someone sees you, a man who understands, eating in some temple of an idol; his own conscience, even if it is weak, may encourage him to eat food which has been offered to idols. ¹¹In this way your knowledge could become the ruin of someone weak, of a brother for whom Christ died. ¹²By sinning in this way against your brothers, and injuring their weak consciences, it would be Christ against whom you sinned. ¹³That is why, since food can be the occasion of my brother's downfall, I shall never eat meat again in case I am the cause of a brother's downfall.

Paul invokes his own example

9 [1]I, personally, am free: I am an apostle and I have seen Jesus our Lord. You are all my work in the Lord. [2]Even if I were not an apostle to others, I should still be an apostle to you who are the seal of my apostolate in the Lord. [3]My answer to those who want to interrogate me is this: [4]Have we not every right to eat and drink?[a] [5]And the right to take a Christian woman round with us, like all the other apostles and the brothers of the Lord and Cephas? [6]Are Barnabas and I the only ones who are not allowed to stop working? [7]Nobody ever paid money to stay in the army, and nobody ever planted a vineyard and refused to eat the fruit of it. Who had there ever been that kept a flock and did not feed on the milk from his flock?

[8]These may be only human comparisons, but does not the Law itself say the same thing? [9]It is written in the Law of Moses: *You must not put a muzzle on the ox when it is treading out the corn.*[b] Is it about oxen that God is concerned, [10]or is there not an obvious reference to ourselves? Clearly this was written for our sake to show that the ploughman ought to plough in expectation, and the thresher to thresh in the expectation of getting his share. [11]If we have sown spiritual things for you, why should you be surprised if we harvest your material things? [12]Others are allowed these rights over

---

[9a.] At the expense of the Christian congregations.   [9b.] Dt 25:4.

you and our right is surely greater? In fact we have never exercised this right. On the contrary we have put up with anything rather than obstruct the Good News of Christ in any way. [13]Remember that the ministers serving in the Temple get their food from the Temple and those serving at the altar can claim their share from the altar itself. [14]In the same sort of way the Lord directed that those who preach the gospel should get their living from the gospel.

[15]However, I have not exercised any of these rights, and I am not writing all this to secure this treatment for myself. I would rather die than let anyone take away something that I can boast of. [16]Not that I do boast of preaching the gospel, since it is a duty which has been laid on me; I should be punished if I did not preach it! [17]If I had chosen this work myself, I might have been paid for it, but as I have not, it is a responsibility which has been put into my hands. [18]Do you know what my reward is? It is this: in my preaching, to be able to offer the Good News free, and not insist on the rights which the gospel gives me.

[19]So though I am not a slave of any man I have made myself the slave of everyone so as to win as many as I could. [20]I made myself a Jew to the Jews, to win the Jews; that is, I who am not a subject of the Law made myself a subject of the Law to those who are the subjects of the Law, to win those who are subject to the

Law. [21]To those who have no Law, I was free of the Law myself (though not free from God's law, being under the law of Christ) to win those who have no Law. [22]For the weak I made myself weak. I made myself all things to all men in order to save some at any cost; [23]and I still do this, for the sake of the gospel, to have a share in its blessings.

[24]All the runners at the stadium are trying to win, but only one of them gets the prize. You must run in the same way, meaning to win. [25]All the fighters at the games go into strict training; they do this just to win a wreath that will wither away, but we do it for a wreath that will never wither. [26]That is how I run, intent on winning; that is how I fight, not beating the air. [27]I treat my body hard and make it obey me, for, having been an announcer myself, I should not want to be disqualified.

A warning, and the lessons of Israel's history

10 [1]I want to remind you, brothers, how our fathers were all guided by a cloud above them and how they all passed through the sea. [2]They were all baptised into Moses in this cloud and in this sea; [3]all ate the same spiritual food [4]and all drank the same spiritual drink, since they all drank from the spiritual rock that followed them as they went, and that rock was Christ. [5]In spite of this, most of them failed to please God and their corpses littered the desert.

⁶These things all happened as warnings[a] for us, not to have the wicked lusts for forbidden things that they had. ⁷Do not become idolaters as some of them did, for scripture says: *After sitting down to eat and drink, the people got up to amuse themselves.*[b] ⁸We must never fall into sexual immorality: some of them did, and twenty-three thousand met their downfall in one day. ⁹We are not to put the Lord to the test: some of them did, and they were killed by snakes. ¹⁰You must never complain: some of them did, and they were killed by the Destroyer.

¹¹All this happened to them as a warning, and it was written down to be a lesson for us who are living at the end of the age. ¹²The man who thinks he is safe must be careful that he does not fall. ¹³The trials that you have had to bear are no more than people normally have. You can trust God not to let you be tried beyond your strength, and with any trial he will give you a way out of it and the strength to bear it.

Sacrificial feasts. No compromise with idolatry

¹⁴This is the reason, my dear brothers, why you must keep clear of idolatry. ¹⁵I say to you as sensible people: judge for yourselves what I am saying. ¹⁶The blessing-cup that we bless is a communion with the blood of Christ,

---

10 a. Lit. 'types'; events prefiguring in the history of Israel the spiritual realities of the messianic age. 10 b. Ex 32:6.

and the bread that we break is a communion with the body of Christ. [17]The fact that there is only one loaf means that, though there are many of us, we form a single body because we all have a share in this one loaf. [18]Look at the other Israel, the race, where those who eat the sacrifices are in communion with the altar. [19]Does this mean that the food sacrificed to idols has a real value, or that the idol itself is real? [20]Not at all. It simply means that the sacrifices that they offer *they sacrifice to demons who are not God.*[c] I have no desire to see you in communion with demons. [21]You cannot drink the cup of the Lord and the cup of demons. You cannot take your share at the table of the Lord and at the table of demons. [22]Do we want to make the Lord angry; are we stronger than he is?

Food sacrificed to idols. Practical solutions

[23]'For me there are no forbidden things', but not everything does good. True, there are no forbidden things, but it is not everything that helps the building to grow. [24]Nobody should be looking for his own advantage, but everybody for the other man's. [25]Do not hesitate to eat anything that is sold in butchers' shops: there is no need to raise questions of conscience; [26]for *the earth and everything that is in it belong to the Lord.*[d] [27]If an unbeliever invites you to his house, go if you want to, and

---

[10 c.] Dt 32:17.   [10 d.] Ps 24:1.

eat whatever is put in front of you, without asking questions just to satisfy conscience. [28]But if someone says to you, 'This food was offered in sacrifice', then, out of consideration for the man that told you, you should not eat it, for the sake of his scruples; [29]his scruples, you see, not your own. Why should my freedom depend on somebody else's conscience? [30]If I take my share with thankfulness, why should I be blamed for food for which I have thanked God?

Conclusion

[31]Whatever you eat, whatever you drink, whatever you do at all, do it for the glory of God. [32]Never do anything offensive to anyone - to Jews or Greeks or to the Church of God; [33]just as I try to be helpful to everyone at all times, not anxious for my own advantage but for the advantage of everybody else, so that they may be saved.

11 [1]Take me for your model, as I take Christ.

C. DECORUM IN PUBLIC WORSHIP

Women's behaviour at services

[2]You have done well in remembering me so constantly and in maintaining the traditions just as I passed them on to you. [3]However, what I want you to understand is that Christ is the head of every man, man is the head of woman, and God is the head of Christ. [4]For a man to pray or prophesy with his head covered is a sign of disrespect

to his head.[a] [5]For a woman, however, it is a sign of disrespect to her head[b] if she prays or prophesies unveiled; she might as well have her hair shaved off. [6]In fact, a woman who will not wear a veil ought to have her hair cut off. If a woman is ashamed to have her hair cut off or shaved, she ought to wear a veil.

[7]A man should certainly not cover his head, since he is the image of God and reflects God's glory; but woman is the reflection of man's glory. [8]For man did not come from woman; no, woman came from man; [9]and man was not created for the sake of woman, but woman was created for the sake of man. [10]That is the argument for women's covering their heads with a symbol of the authority over them, out of respect for the angels[c]. [11]However, though woman cannot do without man, neither can man do without woman, in the Lord; [12]woman may come from man, but man is born of woman - both come from God.

[13]Ask yourselves if it is fitting for a woman to pray to God without a veil; [14]and whether nature itself does not tell you that long hair on a man is nothing to be admired, [15]while a woman, who was given her hair as a covering, thinks long hair her glory?

[16]To anyone who might still want to argue: it is not the custom with us, nor in the churches of God.

11[a]. His leader, a Greek pun.   11[b]. Her husband, who is her head; she is claiming equality.   11[c]. The guardians of due order in public worship.

The Lord's Supper

[17]Now that I am on the subject of instructions, I cannot say that you have done well in holding meetings that do you more harm than good. [18]In the first place, I hear that when you all come together as a community, there are separate factions among you, and I half believe it - [19]since there must no doubt be separate groups among you, to distinguish those who are to be trusted. [20]The point is, when you hold these meetings, it is not the Lord's Supper[d] that you are eating, [21]since when the time comes to eat, everyone is in such a hurry to start his own supper that one person goes hungry while another is getting drunk. [22]Surely you have homes for eating and drinking in? Surely you have enough respect for the community of God not to make poor people embarrassed? What am I to say to you? Congratulate you? I cannot congratulate you on this.

[23]For this is what I received from the Lord, and in turn passed on to you: that on the same night that he was betrayed, the Lord Jesus took some bread, [24]and thanked God for it and broke it, and he said, 'This is my body, which is for you; do this as a memorial of me'. [25]In the same way he took the cup after supper, and said, 'This cup is the new covenant in my blood. Whenever you drink it, do this as a memorial of me.' [26]Until the Lord

[11 d.] The *agapé*, or love feast, preceding the liturgical meal.

comes, therefore, every time you eat this bread and drink this cup, you are proclaiming his death, [27]and so anyone who eats the bread or drinks the cup of the Lord unworthily will be behaving unworthily towards the body and blood of the Lord.

[28]Everyone is to recollect himself before eating this bread and drinking this cup; [29]because a person who eats and drinks without recognising the Body is eating and drinking his own condemnation. [30]In fact that is why many of you are weak and ill and some of you have died. [31]If only we recollected ourselves, we should not be punished like that. [32]But when the Lord does punish us like that, it is to correct us and stop us from being condemned with the world.

[33]So to sum up, my dear brothers, when you meet for the Meal, wait for one another. [34]Anyone who is hungry should eat at home, and then your meeting will not bring your condemnation. The other matters I shall adjust when I come.

Spiritual gifts

12 [1]Now my dear brothers, I want to clear up a wrong impression about spiritual gifts. [2]You remember that, when you were pagans, whenever you felt irresistibly drawn, it was towards dumb idols? [3]It is for that reason that I want you to understand that on the one hand no one can be speaking under the influence of the

Holy Spirit and say, 'Curse Jesus', and on the other hand, no one can say, 'Jesus is Lord' unless he is under the influence of the Holy Spirit.

The variety and the unity of gifts

[4]There is a variety of gifts but always the same Spirit; [5]there are all sorts of service to be done, but always to the same Lord; [6]working in all sorts of different ways in different people, it is the same God who is working in all of them. [7]The particular way in which the Spirit is given to each person is for a good purpose. [8]One may have the gift of preaching with wisdom given him by the Spirit; another may have the gift of preaching instruction given him by the same Spirit; [9]and another the gift of faith given by the same Spirit; another again the gift of healing, through this one Spirit; [10]one, the power of miracles; another, prophecy; another the gift of recognising spirits; another the gift of tongues and another the ability to interpret them. [11]All these are the work of one and the same Spirit, who distributes different gifts to different people just as he chooses.

The analogy of the body

[12]Just as a human body, though it is made up of many parts, is a single unit because all these parts, though many, make one body, so it is with Christ. [13]In the one Spirit we were all baptised, Jews as well as Greeks, slaves as well as citizens, and one Spirit was given to us all to drink.

[14]Nor is the body to be identified with any one of its many parts. [15]If the foot were to say, 'I am not a hand and so I do not belong to the body', would that mean that it stopped being part of the body? [16]If the ear were to say, 'I am not an eye, and so I do not belong to the body', would that mean that it was not a part of the body? [17]If your whole body was just one eye, how would you hear anything? If it was just one ear, how would you smell anything?

[18]Instead of that, God put all the separate parts into the body on purpose. [19]If all the parts were the same, how could it be a body? [20]As it is, the parts are many but the body is one. [21]The eye cannot say to the hand, 'I do not need you', nor can the head say to the feet, 'I do not need you'.

[22]What is more, it is precisely the parts of the body that seem to be the weakest which are the indispensable ones; [23]and it is the least honourable parts of the body that we clothe with the greatest care. So our more improper parts get decorated [24]in a way that our more proper parts do not need. God has arranged the body so that more dignity is given to the parts which are without it, [25]and that there may not be disagreements inside the body, but that each part may be equally concerned for all the others. [26]If one part is hurt, all parts are hurt with it. If one part is given special honour, all parts enjoy it.

[27]Now you together are Christ's body; but each of you is a different part of it. [28]In the Church, God has given the first place to apostles, the second to prophets, the third to

teachers; after them, miracles, and after them the gift of healing; helpers, good leaders, those with many languages. [29]Are all of them apostles, or all of them prophets, or all of them teachers? Do they all have the gift of miracles, [30]or all have the gift of healing? Do all speak strange languages, and all interpret them?

The order of importance in spiritual gifts. Love

[31]Be ambitious for the higher gifts. And I am going to show you a way that is better than any of them.

13 [1]If I have all the eloquence of men or of angels, but speak without love, I am simply a gong booming or a cymbal clashing. [2]If I have the gift of prophecy, understanding all the mysteries there are, and knowing everything, and if I have faith in all its fulness, to move mountains, but without love, then I am nothing at all. [3]If I give away all that I possess, piece by piece, and if I even let them take my body to burn it, but am without love, it will do me no good whatever.

[4]Love is always patient and kind; it is never jealous; love is never boastful or conceited; [5]it is never rude or selfish; it does not take offence, and is not resentful. [6]Love takes no pleasure in other people's sins but delights in the truth; [7]it is always ready to excuse, to trust, to hope, and to endure whatever comes.

[8]Love does not come to an end. But if there are gifts of prophecy, the time will come when they must fail; or the

gift of languages, it will not continue for ever; and knowledge - for this, too, the time will come when it must fail. ⁹For our knowledge is imperfect and our prophesying is imperfect; ¹⁰but once perfection comes, all imperfect things will disappear. ¹¹When I was a child, I used to talk like a child, and think like a child, and argue like a child, but now I am a man, all childish ways are put behind me. ¹²Now we are seeing a dim reflection in a mirror; but then we shall be seeing face to face. The knowledge that I have now is imperfect; but then I shall know as fully as I am known.

¹³In short, there are three things that last: faith, hope and love; and the greatest of these is love.

Spiritual gifts: their respective importance in the community

14 ¹You must want love more than anything else; but still hope for the spiritual gifts as well, especially prophecy. ²Anybody with the gift of tongues speaks to God, but not to other people; because nobody understands him when he talks in the spirit about mysterious things. ³On the other hand, the man who prophesies does talk to other people, to their improvement, their encouragement and their consolation. ⁴The one with the gift of tongues talks for his own benefit, but the man who prophesies does so for the benefit of the community. ⁵While I should like you all to have the gift of tongues, I would much rather you could prophesy, since the man who prophesies

is of greater importance than the man with the gift of tongues, unless of course the latter offers an interpretation so that the church may get some benefit.

⁶Now suppose, my dear brothers, I am someone with the gift of tongues, and I come to visit you, what use shall I be if all my talking reveals nothing new, tells you nothing, and neither inspires you nor instructs you? ⁷Think of a musical instrument, a flute or a harp: if one note on it cannot be distinguished from another, how can you tell what tune is being played? ⁸Or if no one can be sure which call the trumpet has sounded, who will be ready for the attack? ⁹It is the same with you: if your tongue does not produce intelligible speech, how can anyone know what you are saying? You will be talking to the air. ¹⁰There are any number of different languages in the world, and not one of them is meaningless, ¹¹but if I am ignorant of what the sounds mean, I am a savage to the man who is speaking, and he is a savage to me. ¹²It is the same in your own case: since you aspire to spiritual gifts, concentrate on those which will grow to benefit the community.

¹³That is why anybody who has the gift of tongues must pray for the power of interpreting them. ¹⁴For if I use this gift in my prayers, my spirit may be praying but my mind is left barren. ¹⁵What is the answer to that? Surely I should pray not only with the spirit but with the mind as well? And sing praises not only with the spirit but with the mind as well? ¹⁶Any uninitiated person will

never be able to say Amen to your thanksgiving, if you only bless God with the spirit, for he will have no idea what you are saying. [17]However well you make your thanksgiving, the other gets no benefit from it. [18]I thank God that I have a greater gift of tongues than all of you, [19]but when I am in the presence of the community I would rather say five words that mean something than ten thousand words in a tongue.

[20]Brothers, you are not to be childish in your outlook. You can be babies as far as wickedness is concerned, but mentally you must be adult. [21]In the written Law it says: *Through men speaking strange languages and through the lips of foreigners, I shall talk to the nation, and still they will not listen to me, says the Lord.*[a] [22]You see then, that the strange languages are meant to be a sign not for believers but for unbelievers, while on the other hand, prophecy is a sign not for unbelievers but for believers. [23]So that any uninitiated people or unbelievers, coming into a meeting of the whole church where everybody was speaking in tongues, would say you were all mad; [24]but if you were all prophesying and an unbeliever or uninitiated person came in, he would find himself analysed and judged by everyone speaking; [25]he would find his secret thoughts laid bare, and then fall on his face and worship God, declaring that *God is among you indeed.*[b]

[14a.] A free version of Is 28:11-12.   [14b.] Is 45:14.

Regulating spiritual gifts

²⁶So, my dear brothers, what conclusion is to be drawn? At all your meetings, let everyone be ready with a psalm or a sermon or a revelation, or ready to use his gift of tongues or to give an interpretation; but it must always be for the common good. ²⁷If there are people present with the gift of tongues, let only two or three, at the most, be allowed to use it, and only one at a time, and there must be someone to interpret. ²⁸If there is no interpreter present, they must keep quiet in church and speak only to themselves and to God. ²⁹As for prophets, let two or three of them speak, and the others attend to them. ³⁰If one of the listeners receives a revelation, then the man who is already speaking should stop. ³¹For you can all prophesy in turn, so that everybody will learn something and everybody will be encouraged. ³²Prophets can always control their prophetic spirits, ³³since God is not a God of disorder but of peace.

As in all the churches of the saints, ³⁴women are to remain quiet at meetings since they have no permission to speak; they must keep in the background as the Law itself lays it down. ³⁵If they have any questions to ask, they should ask their husbands at home: it does not seem right for a woman to raise her voice at meetings.

³⁶Do you think the word of God came out of yourselves? Or that it has come only to you? ³⁷Anyone who claims to be a prophet or inspired ought to

recognise that what I am writing to you is a command from the Lord. ³⁸Unless he recognises this, you should not recognise him.

³⁹And so, my dear brothers, by all means be ambitious to prophesy, do not suppress the gift of tongues, ⁴⁰but let everything be done with propriety and in order.

III. THE RESURRECTION OF THE DEAD

The fact of the resurrection

15 ¹Brothers, I want to remind you of the gospel I preached to you, the gospel that you received and in which you are firmly established; ²because the gospel will save you only if you keep believing exactly what I preached to you - believing anything else will not lead to anything.

³Well then, in the first place, I taught you what I had been taught myself, namely that Christ died for our sins, in accordance with the scriptures; ⁴that he was buried; and that he was raised to life on the third day, in accordance with the scriptures; ⁵that he appeared first to Cephas and secondly to the Twelve. ⁶Next he appeared to more than five hundred of the brothers at the same time, most of whom are still alive, though some have died; ⁷then he appeared to James, and then to all the apostles; ⁸and last of all he appeared to me too; it was as though I was born when no one expected it.

⁹I am the least of the apostles; in fact, since I persecuted the Church of God, I hardly deserve the name apostle; ¹⁰but by God's grace that is what I am, and the grace that he gave me has not been fruitless. On the contrary, I, or rather the grace of God that is with me, have worked harder than any of the others; ¹¹but what matters is that I preach what they preach, and this is what you all believed.

¹²Now if Christ raised from the dead is what has been preached, how can some of you be saying that there is no resurrection of the dead? ¹³If there is no resurrection of the dead, Christ himself cannot have been raised, ¹⁴and if Christ has not been raised then our preaching is useless and your believing it is useless; ¹⁵indeed, we are shown up as witnesses who have committed perjury before God, because we swore in evidence before God that he had raised Christ to life. ¹⁶For if the dead are not raised, Christ has not been raised, ¹⁷and if Christ has not been raised, you are still in your sins. ¹⁸And what is more serious, all who have died in Christ have perished. ¹⁹If our hope in Christ has been for this life only, we are the most unfortunate of all people.

²⁰But Christ has in fact been raised from the dead, the first-fruits of all who have fallen asleep. ²¹Death came through one man and in the same way the resurrection of the dead has come through one man. ²²Just as all men die in Adam, so all men will be brought to life in Christ; ²³but

all of them in their proper order: Christ as the first-fruits and then, after the coming of Christ, those who belong to him. [24]After that will come the end, when he hands over the kingdom to God the Father, having done away with every sovereignty, authority and power. [25]For he must be king *until he has put all his enemies under his feet*[a] [26]and the last of the enemies to be destroyed is death, for everything is to be *put under his feet*. [27]- Though when it is said that *everything is subjected*, this clearly cannot include the One who subjected everything to him. [28]And when everything is subjected to him, then the Son himself will be subject in his turn to the One who subjected all things to him, so that God may be all in all.

[29]If this were not true, what do people hope to gain by being baptised for the dead? If the dead are not ever going to be raised, why be baptised on their behalf? [30]What about ourselves? Why are we living under a constant threat? [31]I face death every day, brothers, and I can swear it by the pride that I take in you in Christ Jesus our Lord. [32]If my motives were only human ones, what good would it do me to fight the wild animals at Ephesus? [33]You say: *Let us eat and drink today; tomorrow we shall be dead*.[b] You must stop being led astray: 'Bad friends ruin the noblest people'.[c] [34]Come to

---

15[a]. Ps 110:1.   15[b]. Is 22:13.   15[c]. This quotation from Menander's *Thais* may have become a proverb.

your senses, behave properly, and leave sin alone; there are some of you who seem not to know God at all; you should be ashamed.

The manner of the resurrection

[35]Someone may ask, 'How are dead people raised, and what sort of body do they have when they come back?' [36]They are stupid questions. Whatever you sow in the ground has to die before it is given new life [37]and the thing that you sow is not what is going to come; you sow a bare grain, say of wheat or something like that, [38]and then God gives it the sort of body that he has chosen: each sort of seed gets its own sort of body.

[39]Everything that is flesh is not the same flesh: there is human flesh, animals' flesh, the flesh of birds and the flesh of fish. [40]Then there are heavenly bodies and there are earthly bodies; but the heavenly bodies have a beauty of their own and the earthly bodies a different one. [41]The sun has its brightness, the moon a different brightness, and the stars a different brightness, and the stars differ from each other in brightness. [42]It is the same with the resurrection of the dead: the thing that is sown is perishable but what is raised is imperishable; [43]the thing that is sown is contemptible but what is raised is glorious; the thing that is sown is weak but what is raised is powerful; [44]when it is sown it embodies the soul, when it is raised it embodies the spirit.

If the soul has its own embodiment, so does the spirit have its own embodiment. [45]The first *man*, Adam, as scripture says, *became a living soul*; but the last Adam has become a life-giving spirit. [46]That is, first the one with the soul, not the spirit, and after that, the one with the spirit. [47]The first man, being from the earth, is earthly by nature; the second man is from heaven. [48]As this earthly man was, so are we on earth; and as the heavenly man is, so are we in heaven. [49]And we, who have been modelled on the earthly man, will be modelled on the heavenly man.

[50]Or else, brothers, put it this way: flesh and blood cannot inherit the kingdom of God: and the perishable cannot inherit what lasts for ever. [51]I will tell you something that has been secret: that we are not all going to die, but we shall all be changed. [52]This will be instantaneous, in the twinkling of an eye, when the last trumpet sounds. It will sound, and the dead will be raised, imperishable, and we shall be changed as well, [53]because our present perishable nature must put on imperishability and this mortal nature must put on immortality.

A hymn of triumph. Conclusion

[54]When this perishable nature has put on imperishability, and when this mortal nature has put on immortality, then the words of scripture will come true: *Death is swallowed up in victory.* [55]*Death, where is your*

victory? Death, where is your sting?[d] [56]Now the sting of death is sin, and sin gets its power from the Law. [57]So let us thank God for giving us the victory through our Lord Jesus Christ.

[58]Never give in then, my dear brothers, never admit defeat; keep on working at the Lord's work always, knowing that, in the Lord, you cannot be labouring in vain.

CONCLUSION

Commendations. Greetings

16 [1]Now about the collection made for the saints: you are to do as I told the churches in Galatia to do. [2]Every Sunday, each one of you must put aside what he can afford, so that collections need not be made after I have come. [3]When I am with you, I will send your offering to Jerusalem by the hand of whatever men you give letters of reference to; [4]If it seems worth while for me to go too, they can travel with me.

[5]I shall be coming to you after I have passed through Macedonia - and I am doing no more than pass through Macedonia - [6]and I may be staying with you, perhaps even passing the winter, to make sure that it is you who send me on my way wherever my travels take me. [7]As you see, I do not want to make it

---

[15 d]. A free version; see Ho 13:14.

only a passing visit to you and I hope to spend some time with you, the Lord permitting. [8]In any case I shall be staying at Ephesus until Pentecost [9]because a big and important door has opened for my work and there is a great deal of opposition.

[10]If Timothy comes, show him that he has nothing to be afraid of in you: like me, he is doing the Lord's work, [11]and nobody is to be scornful of him. Send him happily on his way to come back to me; the brothers and I are waiting for him. [12]As for our brother Apollos, I begged him to come to you with the brothers but he was quite firm that he did not want to go yet and he will come as soon as he can.

[13]Be awake to all the dangers; stay firm in the faith; be brave and be strong. [14]Let everything you do be done in love.

[15]There is something else to ask you, brothers. You know how the Stephanas family, who were the first-fruits of Achaia, have really worked hard to help the saints. [16]Well, I want you in your turn to put yourselves at the service of people like this, and anyone who helps and works with them. [17]I am delighted that Stephanas, Fortunatus and Achaicus have arrived; they make up for your absence. [18]They have settled my mind, and yours too; I hope you appreciate men like this.

¹⁹All the churches of Asia send you greetings. Aquila and Prisca, with the church that meets at their house, send you their warmest wishes, in the Lord. ²⁰All the brothers send you their greetings. Greet one another with a holy kiss.

²¹This greeting is in my own hand - Paul.

²²If anyone does not love the Lord, a curse on him. 'Maran atha.'[a]

²³The grace of the Lord Jesus be with you.

²⁴My love is with you all in Christ Jesus.

16a. Aramaic. 'The Lord is coming', or 'Lord, come'.

❧ 2 CORINTHIANS ❧

THE SECOND LETTER OF PAUL TO THE CHURCH AT CORINTH

INTRODUCTION

Address and greetings. Thanksgiving

1 ¹From Paul, appointed by God to be an apostle of Christ Jesus, and from Timothy, one of the brothers, to the church of God at Corinth and to all the saints in the whole of Achaia. ²Grace and peace to you from God our Father and the Lord Jesus Christ.

³Blessed be the God and Father of our Lord Jesus Christ, a gentle Father and the God of all consolation, ⁴who comforts us in all our sorrows, so that we can offer others, in their sorrows, the consolation that we have received from God ourselves. ⁵Indeed, as the sufferings of Christ overflow to us, so, through Christ, does our consolation overflow. ⁶When we are made to suffer, it is for your consolation and salvation. When, instead, we are comforted, this should be a consolation to you, supporting you in patiently bearing the same sufferings as we bear. ⁷And our hope for you is confident, since we

know that, sharing our sufferings, you will also share our consolations.

[8]For we should like you to realise, brothers, that the things we had to undergo in Asia were more of a burden than we could carry, so that we despaired of coming through alive. [9]Yes, we were carrying our own death warrant with us, and it has taught us not to rely on ourselves but only on God, who raises the dead to life. [10]And he saved us from dying, as he will save us again; yes, that is our firm hope in him, that in the future he will save us again. [11]You must all join in the prayers for us: the more people there are asking for help for us, the more will be giving thanks when it is granted to us.

I. SOME RECENT EVENTS REVIEWED

Why Paul changed his plans

[12]There is one thing we are proud of, and our conscience tells us it is true: that we have always treated everybody, and especially you, with the reverence and sincerity which come from God, and by the grace of God we have done this without ulterior motives. [13]There are no hidden meanings in our letters besides what you can read for yourselves and understand. [14]And I hope that, although you do not know us very well yet, you will have come to recognise, when the day of our Lord Jesus comes, that you can be as proud of us as we are of you.

¹⁵Because I was so sure of this, I had meant to come to you first, so that you would benefit doubly; ¹⁶staying with you before going to Macedonia and coming back to you again on the way back from Macedonia, for you to see me on my way to Judaea. ¹⁷Do you think I was not sure of my own intentions when I planned this? Do you really think that when I am making my plans, my motives are ordinary human ones, and that I say Yes, yes, and No, no, at the same time? ¹⁸I swear by God's truth, there is no Yes and No about what we say to you. ¹⁹The Son of God, the Christ Jesus that we proclaimed among you - I mean Silvanus and Timothy and I - was never Yes and No: with him it was always Yes, ²⁰and however many the promises God made, the Yes to them all is in him. That is why it is 'through him' that we answer Amen to the praise of God. ²¹Remember it is God himself who assures us all, and you, of our standing in Christ, and has anointed us, ²²marking us with his seal and giving us the pledge, the Spirit, that we carry in our hearts.

²³By my life, I call God to witness that the reason why I did not come to Corinth after all was to spare your feelings. ²⁴We are not dictators over your faith, but are fellow workers with you for your happiness; in the faith you are steady enough. **2** ¹Well then, I made up my mind not to pay you a second distressing visit. ²I may have hurt you, but if so I have hurt the only people who could give me any pleasure. ³I wrote as I did to make sure that, when

I came, I should not be distressed by the very people who should have made me happy. I am sure you all know that I could never be happy unless you were. ⁴When I wrote to you, in deep distress and anguish of mind, and in tears, it was not to make you feel hurt but to let you know how much love I have for you.

⁵Someone has been the cause of pain; and the cause of pain not to me, but to some degree - not to overstate it - to all of you. ⁶The punishment already imposed by the majority on the man in question is enough; ⁷and the best thing now is to give him your forgiveness and encouragement, or he might break down from so much misery. ⁸So I am asking you to give some definite proof of your love for him. ⁹What I really wrote for, after all, was to test you and see whether you are completely obedient. ¹⁰Anybody that you forgive, I forgive; and as for my forgiving anything - if there has been anything to be forgiven, I have forgiven it for your sake in the presence of Christ. ¹¹And so we will not be outwitted by Satan - we know well enough what his intentions are.

From Troas to Macedonia. The apostolate: its importance

¹²When I went up to Troas to preach the Good News of Christ, and the door was wide open for my work there in the Lord, ¹³I was so continually uneasy in mind at not meeting brother Titus there, I said good-bye to them and went on to Macedonia.

[14]Thanks be to God who, wherever he goes, makes us, in Christ, partners of his triumph,[a] and through us is spreading the knowledge of himself, like a sweet smell, everywhere. [15]We are Christ's incense to God for those who are being saved and for those who are not; [16]for the last, the smell of death that leads to death, for the first the sweet smell of life that leads to life. And who could be qualified for work like this? [17]At least we do not go round offering the word of God for sale, as many other people do. In Christ, we speak as men of sincerity, as envoys of God and in God's presence.

3 [1]Does this sound like a new attempt to commend ourselves to you? Unlike other people, we need no letters of recommendation either to you or from you, [2]because you are yourselves our letter, written in our hearts, that anybody can see and read, [3]and it is plain that you are a letter from Christ, drawn up by us, and written not with ink but with the Spirit of the living God, not on stone tablets but on the tablets of your living hearts.

[4]Before God, we are confident of this through Christ: [5]not that we are qualified in ourselves to claim anything as our own work: all our qualifications come from God. [6]He is the one who has given us the qualifications to be the administrators of this new covenant, which is not a covenant of written letters but of the Spirit: the written

---

[2a.] Like a victorious general making his ceremonial entry into Rome.

letters bring death, but the Spirit gives life. [7]Now if the administering of death, in the written letters engraved on stones, was accompanied by such a brightness that the Israelites could not bear looking at the face of Moses, though it was a brightness that faded, [8]then how much greater will be the brightness that surrounds the administering of the Spirit! [9]For if there was any splendour in administering condemnation, there must be very much greater splendour in administering justification. [10]In fact, compared with this greater splendour, the thing that used to have such splendour now seems to have none; [11]and if what was so temporary had any splendour, there must be much more in what is going to last for ever.

[12]Having this hope, we can be quite confident; [13]not like Moses, who put a veil over his face so that the Israelites would not notice the ending of what had to fade.[a] [14]And anyway, their minds had been dulled; indeed, to this very day, that same veil is still there when the old covenant is being read, a veil never lifted, since Christ alone can remove it. [15]Yes, even today, whenever Moses is read, the veil is over their minds. [16]It will not be removed until they turn to the Lord. [17]Now this Lord is the Spirit, and where the Spirit of the Lord is, there is freedom. [18]And we, with our unveiled faces reflecting like mirrors the brightness of

---

[3a] See Ex 34:33.

the Lord, all grow brighter and brighter as we are turned into the image that we reflect; this is the work of the Lord who is Spirit.

4 ¹Since we have by an act of mercy been entrusted with this work of administration, there is no weakening on our part. ²On the contrary, we will have none of the reticence of those who are ashamed, no deceitfulness or watering down the word of God; but the way we commend ourselves to every human being with a conscience is by stating the truth openly in the sight of God. ³If our gospel does not penetrate the veil, then the veil is on those who are not on the way to salvation; ⁴the unbelievers whose minds the god of this world has blinded, to stop them seeing the light shed by the Good News of the glory of Christ, who is the image of God. ⁵For it is not ourselves that we are preaching, but Christ Jesus as the Lord, and ourselves as your servants for Jesus' sake. ⁶It is the same God that said, 'Let there be light shining out of darkness', who has shone in our minds to radiate the light of the knowledge of God's glory, the glory on the face of Christ.

The trials and hopes of the apostolate

⁷We are only the earthenware jars that hold this treasure, to make it clear that such an overwhelming power comes from God and not from us. ⁸We are in difficulties on all sides, but never cornered; we see no answer to our

problems, but never despair; [9]we have been persecuted, but never deserted; knocked down, but never killed; [10]always, wherever we may be, we carry with us in our body the death of Jesus, so that the life of Jesus, too, may always be seen in our body. [11]Indeed, while we are still alive, we are consigned to our death every day, for the sake of Jesus, so that in our mortal flesh the life of Jesus, too, may be openly shown. [12]So death is at work in us, but life in you.

[13]But as we have the same spirit of faith that is mentioned in scripture - *I believed, and therefore I spoke*[a] - we too believe and therefore we too speak, [14]knowing that he who raised the Lord Jesus to life will raise us with Jesus in our turn, and put us by his side and you with us. [15]You see, all this is for your benefit, so that the more grace is multiplied among people, the more thanksgiving there will be, to the glory of God.

[16]That is why there is no weakening on our part, and instead, though this outer man of ours may be falling into decay, the inner man is renewed day by day. [17]Yes, the troubles which are soon over, though they weigh little, train us for the carrying of a weight of eternal glory which is out of all proportion to them. [18]And so we have no eyes for things that are visible, but only for things that are invisible; for visible things last only for a time, and the invisible things are eternal.

[4a.] Ps 116:10.

5 ¹For we know that when the tent that we live in on earth is folded up, there is a house built by God for us, an everlasting home not made by human hands, in the heavens. ²In this present state, it is true, we groan as we wait with longing to put on our heavenly home over the other; ³we should like to be found wearing clothes and not without them. ⁴Yes, we groan and find it a burden being still in this tent, not that we want to strip it off, but to put the second garment over it and to have what must die taken up into life. ⁵This is the purpose for which God made us, and he has given us the pledge of the Spirit.

⁶We are always full of confidence, then, when we remember that to live in the body means to be exiled from the Lord, ⁷going as we do by faith and not by sight ⁸- we are full of confidence, I say, and actually want to be exiled from the body and make our home with the Lord. ⁹Whether we are living in the body or exiled from it, we are intent on pleasing him. ¹⁰For all the truth about us will be brought out in the law court of Christ, and each of us will get what he deserves for the things he did in the body, good or bad.

The apostolate in action

¹¹And so it is with the fear of the Lord in mind that we try to win people over. God knows us for what we really are, and I hope that in your consciences you know us too. ¹²This is not another attempt to commend ourselves to

you: we are simply giving you reasons to be proud of us, so that you will have an answer ready for the people who can boast more about what they seem than what they are. [13]If we seemed out of our senses, it was for God; but if we are being reasonable now, it is for your sake. [14]And this is because the love of Christ overwhelms us when we reflect that if one man has died for all, then all men should be dead; [15]and the reason he died for all was so that living men should live no longer for themselves, but for him who died and was raised to life for them.

[16]From now onwards, therefore, we do not judge anyone by the standards of the flesh. Even if we did once know Christ in the flesh, that is not how we know him now. [17]And for anyone who is in Christ, there is a new creation; the old creation has gone, and now the new one is here. [18]It is all God's work. It was God who reconciled us to himself through Christ and gave us the work of handing on this reconciliation. [19]In other words, God in Christ was reconciling the world to himself, not holding men's faults against them, and he has entrusted to us the news that they are reconciled. [20]So we are ambassadors for Christ; it is as though God were appealing through us, and the appeal that we make in Christ's name is: be reconciled to God. [21]For our sake God made the sinless one into sin, so that in him we might become the goodness of God. **6** [1]As his fellow workers, we beg you once again not to neglect the grace of God that you have received. [2]For he

says: *At the favourable time, I have listened to you; on the day of salvation I came to your help.*[a] Well, now is the favourable time; this is the day of salvation.

[3]We do nothing that people might object to, so as not to bring discredit on our function as God's servants. [4]Instead, we prove we are servants of God by great fortitude in times of suffering: in times of hardship and distress; [5]when we are flogged, or sent to prison, or mobbed; labouring, sleepless, starving. [6]We prove we are God's servants by our purity, knowledge, patience and kindness; by a spirit of holiness, by a love free from affectation; [7]by the word of truth and by the power of God; by being armed with the weapons of righteousness in the right hand and in the left, [8]prepared for honour or disgrace, for blame or praise; taken for impostors while we are genuine; [9]obscure yet famous; said to be dying and here are we alive; rumoured to be executed before we are sentenced; [10]thought most miserable and yet we are always rejoicing; taken for paupers though we make others rich, for people having nothing though we have everything.

Paul opens his heart. A warning

[11]Corinthians, we have spoken to you very frankly; our mind has been opened in front of you. [12]Any constraint that you feel is not on our side; the

---

[6a.] Is 49:8.

constraint is in your own selves. [13]I speak as if to children of mine: as a fair exchange, open your minds in the same way.

[14]Do not harness yourselves in an uneven team with unbelievers. Virtue is no companion for crime. Light and darkness have nothing in common. [15]Christ is not the ally of Beliar, nor has a believer anything to share with an unbeliever. [16]The temple of God has no common ground with idols, and that is what we are - the temple of the living God. We have God's word for it: *I will make my home among them and live with them; I will be their God and they shall be my people.*[b] [17]Then *come away from them and keep aloof, says the Lord. Touch nothing that is unclean,*[c] *and I will welcome you* [18]*and be your father, and you shall be my sons and daughters, says the Almighty Lord.*[d]

7 [1]With promises like these made to us, dear brothers, let us wash off all that can soil either body or spirit, to reach perfection of holiness in the fear of God.

[2]Keep a place for us in your hearts. We have not injured anyone, or ruined anyone, or exploited anyone. [3]I am not saying this to put any blame on you; as I have already told you, you are in our hearts - together we live or together we die. [4]I have the very greatest confidence in you, and I am so proud of you that in all our trouble I am filled with consolation and my joy is overflowing.

[6b] Lv 26:11-12.   [6c] Is 52:11.   [6d] Is 43:6.

Paul in Macedonia; he is joined by Titus

⁵Even after we had come to Macedonia, however, there was no rest for this body of ours. Far from it; we found trouble on all sides: quarrels outside, misgivings inside. ⁶But God comforts the miserable, and he comforted us, by the arrival of Titus, ⁷and not only by his arrival but also by the comfort which he had gained from you. He has told us all about how you want to see me, how sorry you were, and how concerned for me, and so I am happier now than I was before.

⁸But to tell the truth, even if I distressed you by my letter, I do not regret it. I did regret it before, and I see that that letter did distress you, at least for a time; ⁹but I am happy now - not because I made you suffer, but because your suffering led to your repentance. Yours has been a kind of suffering that God approves, and so you have come to no kind of harm from us. ¹⁰To suffer in God's way means changing for the better and leaves no regrets, but to suffer as the world knows suffering brings death. ¹¹Just look at what suffering in God's way has brought you: what keenness, what explanations, what indignation, what alarm! Yes, and what aching to see me, what concern for me, and what justice done! In every way you have shown yourselves blameless in this affair. ¹²So then, though I wrote the letter to you, it was not written for the sake either of the offender or of the

one offended; it was to make you realise, in the sight of God, your own concern for us. [13]That is what we have found so encouraging.

With this encouragement, too, we had the even greater happiness of finding Titus so happy; thanks to you all, he has no more worries; [14]I had rather boasted to him about you, and now I have not been made to look foolish; in fact, our boasting to Titus has proved to be as true as anything that we ever said to you. [15]His own personal affection for you is all the greater when he remembers how willing you have all been, and with what deep respect you welcomed him. [16]I am very happy knowing that I can rely on you so completely.

II. ORGANISATION OF THE COLLECTION

Why the Corinthians should be generous

8 [1]Now here, brothers, is the news of the grace of God which was given in the churches in Macedonia; [2]and of how, throughout great trials by suffering, their constant cheerfulness and their intense poverty have overflowed in a wealth of generosity. [3]I can swear that they gave not only as much as they could afford, but far more, and quite spontaneously, [4]begging and begging us for the favour of sharing in this service to the saints [5]and, what was quite unexpected, they offered their own selves first to God and, under God, to us.

⁶Because of this, we have asked Titus, since he has already made a beginning, to bring this work of mercy to the same point of success among you. ⁷You always have the most of everything - of faith, of eloquence, of understanding, of keenness for any cause, and the biggest share of our affection - so we expect you to put the most into this work of mercy too. ⁸It is not an order that I am giving you; I am just testing the genuineness of your love against the keenness of others. ⁹Remember how generous the Lord Jesus was: he was rich, but he became poor for your sake, to make you rich out of his poverty. ¹⁰As I say, I am only making a suggestion; it is only fair to you, since you were the first, a year ago, not only in taking action but even in deciding to. ¹¹So now finish the work and let the results be worthy, as far as you can afford it, of the decision you made promptly. ¹²As long as the readiness is there, a man is acceptable with whatever he can afford; never mind what is beyond his means. ¹³This does not mean that to give relief to others you ought to make things difficult for yourselves: it is a question of balancing ¹⁴what happens to be your surplus now against their present need, and one day they may have something to spare that will supply your own need. That is how we strike a balance: ¹⁵as scripture says: *The man who gathered much had none too much, the man who gathered little did not go short.*[a]

---

[a] Ex 16:18.

The delegates recommended to the Corinthians

[16]I thank God for putting into Titus' heart the same concern for you that I have myself. [17]He did what we asked him; indeed he is more concerned than ever, and is visiting you on his own initiative. [18]As his companion we are sending the brother who is famous in all the churches for spreading the gospel. [19]More than that, he happens to be the same brother who has been elected by the churches to be our companion on this errand of mercy that, for the glory of God, we have undertaken to satisfy our impatience to help. [20]We hope that in this way there will be no accusations made about our administering such a large fund; [21]for *we are trying to do right* not only *in the sight of God* but *also* in the sight of *men*.[b] [22]To accompany these, we are sending a third brother, of whose keenness we have often had proof in many different ways, and who is particularly keen about this, because he has great confidence in you. [23]Titus, perhaps I should add, is my own colleague and fellow worker in your interests; the other two brothers, who are delegates of the churches, are a real glory to Christ. [24]So then, in front of all the churches, give them a proof of your love, and prove to them that we are right to be proud of you.

9 [1]There is really no need for me to write to you on the subject of offering your services to the saints, [2]since I know how anxious you are to help; in fact, I boast about

---

8 b. Pr 3:4 (LXX).

you to the Macedonians, telling them, 'Achaia has been ready since last year'. So your zeal has been a spur to many more. [3]I am sending the brothers all the same, to make sure that our boasting about you does not prove to have been empty this time, and that you really are ready as I said you would be. [4]If some of the Macedonians who are coming with me found you unprepared, we should be humiliated - to say nothing of yourselves - after being so confident. [5]That is why I have thought it necessary to ask these brothers to go on to you ahead of us, and make sure in advance that the gift you promised is all ready, and that it all comes as a gift out of your generosity and not by being extorted from you.

Blessings to be expected from the collection

[6]Do not forget: thin sowing means thin reaping; the more you sow, the more you reap. [7]Each one should give what he has decided in his own mind, not grudgingly or because he is made to, for *God loves a cheerful giver.*[a] [8]And there is no limit to the blessings which God can send you - he will make sure that you will always have all you need for yourselves in every possible circumstance, and still have something to spare for all sorts of good works. [9]As scripture says: *He was free in almsgiving, and gave to the poor: his good deeds will never be forgotten.*[b]

[9a] Pr 22:8 (LXX).   [9b] Ps 112:9.

¹⁰The one who provides *seed for the sower and bread for food* will provide you with all the seed you want and make *the harvest of your good deeds* a larger one, ¹¹and, made richer in every way, you will be able to do all the generous things which, through us, are the cause of thanksgiving to God. ¹²For doing this holy service is not only supplying all the needs of the saints, but it is also increasing the amount of thanksgiving that God receives. ¹³By offering this service, you show them what you are, and that makes them give glory to God for the way you accept and profess the gospel of Christ, and for your sympathetic generosity to them and to all. ¹⁴And their prayers for you, too, show how they are drawn to you on account of all the grace that God has given you. ¹⁵Thanks be to God for his inexpressible gift!

III. PAUL'S APOLOGIA

Paul's reply to accusations of weakness

10 ¹This is a personal matter; this is Paul himself appealing to you by the gentleness and patience of Christ - I, the man who is so humble when he is facing you, but bullies you when he is at a distance. ²I only ask that I do not have to bully you when I come, with all the confident assurance I mean to show when I come face to face with people I could name who think we go by ordinary human motives. ³We live in the flesh, of course,

but the muscles that we fight with are not flesh. [4]Our war is not fought with weapons of flesh, yet they are strong enough, in God's cause, to demolish fortresses. We demolish sophistries, [5]and the arrogance that tries to resist the knowledge of God; every thought is our prisoner, captured to be brought into obedience to Christ. [6]Once you have given your complete obedience, we are prepared to punish any disobedience.

[7]Face plain facts. Anybody who is convinced that he belongs to Christ must go on to reflect that we all belong to Christ no less than he does. [8]Maybe I do boast rather too much about our authority, but the Lord gave it to me for building you up and not for pulling you down, and I shall not be ashamed of it. [9]I do not want you to think of me as someone who only frightens you by letter. [10]Someone said, 'He writes powerful and strongly-worded letters but when he is with you you see only half a man and no preacher at all'. [11]The man who said that can remember this: whatever we are like in the words of our letters when we are absent, that is what we shall be like in our actions when we are present.

His reply to the accusation of ambition

[12]We are not being so bold as to rank ourselves, or invite comparison, with certain people who write their own references. Measuring themselves against themselves, and comparing themselves to themselves,

they are simply foolish. [13]We, on the other hand, are not going to boast without a standard to measure against: taking for our measure the yardstick which God gave us to measure with, which is long enough to reach to you. [14]We are not stretching further than we ought; otherwise we should not have reached you, as we did come all the way to you with the gospel of Christ. [15]So we are not boasting without any measure, about work that was done by other people; in fact, we trust that, as your faith grows, we shall get taller and taller, when judged by our own standard. [16]I mean, we shall be carrying the gospel to places far beyond you, without encroaching on anyone else's field, not boasting of the work already done. [17]*If anyone wants to boast, let him boast of the Lord.*[a] [18]It is not the man who commends himself that can be accepted, but the man who is commended by the Lord.

Paul is driven to sound his own praises

11 [1]I only wish you were able to tolerate a little foolishness from me. But of course: you are tolerant towards me. [2]You see, the jealousy that I feel for you is God's own jealousy: I arranged for you to marry Christ so that I might give you away as a chaste virgin to this one husband. [3]But the serpent, with his cunning, seduced Eve, and I am afraid that in the same way your

---

[10a.] Jr 9:23.

ideas may get corrupted and turned away from simple devotion to Christ. ⁴Because any new-comer has only to proclaim a new Jesus, different from the one that we preached, or you have only to receive a new spirit, different from the one you have already received, or a new gospel, different from the one you have already accepted - and you welcome it with open arms. ⁵As far as I can tell, these arch-apostles have nothing more than I have. ⁶I may not be a polished speechmaker, but as for knowledge, that is a different matter; surely we have made this plain, speaking on every subject in front of all of you.

⁷Or was I wrong, lowering myself so as to lift you high, by preaching the gospel of God to you and taking no fee for it? ⁸I was robbing other churches living on them so that I could serve you. ⁹When I was with you and ran out of money, I was no burden to anyone; the brothers who came from Macedonia provided me with everything I wanted. I was very careful, and I always shall be, not to be a burden to you in any way, ¹⁰and by Christ's truth in me, this cause of boasting will never be taken from me in the regions of Achaia. ¹¹Would I do that if I did not love you? God knows I do. ¹²I intend to go on doing what I am doing now - leaving no opportunity for those people who are looking for an opportunity to claim equality with us in what they boast of. ¹³These people are counterfeit apostles, they are dishonest workmen disguised as

apostles of Christ. [14]There is nothing unexpected about that; if Satan himself goes disguised as an angel of light, is there is no need to be surprised when his servants, too, disguise themselves as the servants of righteousness. They will come to the end that they deserve.

[16]As I said before, let no one take me for a fool; but if you must, then treat me as a fool and let me do a little boasting of my own. [17]What I am going to say now is not prompted by the Lord, but said as if in a fit of folly, in the certainty that I have something to boast about. [18]So many others have been boasting of their worldly achievements, that I will boast myself. [19]You are all wise men and can cheerfully tolerate fools, [20]yes, even to tolerating somebody who makes slaves of you, makes you feed him, imposes on you, orders you about and slaps you in the face. [21]I hope you are ashamed of us for being weak with you instead!

But if anyone wants some brazen speaking - I am still talking as a fool - then I can be as brazen as any of them, and about the same things. [22]Hebrews, are they? So am I. Israelites? So am I. Descendants of Abraham? So am I. [23]The servants of Christ? I must be mad to say this, but so am I, and more than they: more, because I have worked harder, I have been sent to prison more often, and whipped many times more, often almost to death. [24]Five times I had the thirty-nine lashes from the Jews; [25]three times I have been beaten with sticks; once I was stoned;

three times I have been shipwrecked and once adrift in the open sea for a night and a day. [26]Constantly travelling, I have been in danger from rivers and in danger from brigands, in danger from my own people and in danger from pagans; in danger in the towns, in danger in the open country, danger at sea and danger from so-called brothers. [27]I have worked and laboured, often without sleep; I have been hungry and thirsty and often starving; I have been in the cold without clothes. [28]And, to leave out much more, there is my daily preoccupation: my anxiety for all the churches. [29]When any man has had scruples, I have had scruples with him; when any man is made to fall, I am tortured.

[30]If I am to boast, then let me boast of my own feebleness. [31]The God and Father of the Lord Jesus - bless him for ever - knows that I am not lying. [32]When I was in Damascus, the ethnarch of King Aretas put guards round the city to catch me, [33]and I had to be let down over the wall in a hamper, through a window, in order to escape.

12 [1]Must I go on boasting, though there is nothing to be gained by it? But I will move on to the visions and revelations I have had from the Lord. [2]I know a man in Christ who, fourteen years ago, was caught up - whether still in the body or out of the body, I do not know; God knows - right into the third heaven.[a] [3]I do

---

12a. I.e. the highest heaven.

know, however, that this same person - whether in the body or out of the body, I do not know; God knows - ⁴was caught up into paradise and heard things which must not and cannot be put into human language. ⁵I will boast about a man like that, but not about anything of my own except my weaknesses. ⁶If I should decide to boast, I should not be made to look foolish, because I should only be speaking the truth; but I am not going to, in case anyone should begin to think I am better than he can actually see and hear me to be.

⁷In view of the extraordinary nature of these revelations, to stop me from getting too proud I was given a thorn in the flesh, an angel of Satan to beat me and stop me from getting too proud! ⁸About this thing, I have pleaded with the Lord three times for it to leave me, ⁹but he has said, 'My grace is enough for you: my power is at its best in weakness'. So I shall be very happy to make my weaknesses my special boast so that the power of Christ may stay over me, ¹⁰and that is why I am quite content with my weaknesses, and with insults, hardships, persecutions, and the agonies I go through for Christ's sake. For it is when I am weak that I am strong.

¹¹I have been talking like a fool, but you forced me to do it: you are the ones who should have been commending me. Though I am a nobody, there is not a thing these arch-apostles have that I do not have as well. ¹²You have seen done among you all the things that mark

the true apostle, unfailingly produced: the signs, the marvels, the miracles. [13]Is there anything of which you have had less than the other churches have had, except that I have not myself been a burden on you? For this unfairness, please forgive me. [14]I am all prepared now to come to you for the third time, and I am not going to be a burden on you: it is you I want, not your possessions. Children are not expected to save up for their parents, but parents for children. [15]I am perfectly willing to spend what I have, and to be expended, in the interests of your souls. Because I love you more, must I be loved the less?

[16]All very well, you say: I personally put no pressure on you, but like the cunning fellow that I am, I took you in by a trick. [17]So we exploited you, did we, through one of the men that I have sent to you? [18]Well, Titus went at my urging, and I sent the brother that came with him. Can Titus have exploited you? You know that he and I have always been guided by the same spirit and trodden in the same tracks.

Paul's fears and anxieties

[19]All this time you have been thinking that our defence is addressed to you, but it is before God that we, in Christ, are speaking; and it is all, my dear brothers, for your benefit. [20]What I am afraid of is that when I come I may find you different from what I want you to be, and you may find that I am not as you would like me to be;

119

and then there will be wrangling, jealousy, and tempers roused, intrigues and backbiting and gossip, obstinacies and disorder. ²¹I am afraid that on my next visit, my God may make me ashamed on your account and I shall be grieving over all those who sinned before and have still not repented of the impurities, fornication and debauchery they committed.

13 ¹This will be the third time I have come to you. *The evidence of three, or at least two, witnesses is necessary to sustain the charge.*[a] ²I gave warning when I was with you the second time and I give warning now, too, before I come, to those who sinned before and to any others, that when I come again, I shall have no mercy. ³You want proof, you say, that it is Christ speaking in me: you have known him not as a weakling, but as a power among you? ⁴Yes, but he was crucified through weakness, and still he lives now through the power of God. So then, we are weak, as he was, but we shall live with him, through the power of God, for your benefit.

⁵Examine yourselves to make sure you are in the faith; test yourselves. Do you acknowledge that Jesus Christ is really in you? If not, you have failed the test, ⁶but we, as I hope you will come to see, have not failed it. ⁷We pray to God that you will do nothing wrong: not that we want to appear as the ones who have been successful - we would

---

[13a] Dt 19:15.

rather that you did well even though we failed. [8]We have no power to resist the truth; only to further it. [9]We are only too glad to be weak provided you are strong. What we ask in our prayers is for you to be made perfect. [10]That is why I am writing this from a distance, so that when I am with you I shall not need to be strict, with the authority which the Lord gave me for building up and not for destroying.

CONCLUSION

Recommendations. Greetings. Final good wishes

[11]In the meantime, brothers, we wish you happiness; try to grow perfect; help one another. Be united; live in peace, and the God of love and peace will be with you.

[12]Greet one another with the holy kiss. All the saints send you greetings.

[13]The grace of the Lord Jesus Christ, the love of God and the fellowship of the Holy Spirit be with you all.

❧ GALATIANS ❧

THE LETTER OF PAUL TO THE
CHURCH IN GALATIA

Address

1 ¹From Paul to the churches of Galatia, and from all the brothers who are here with me, ²an apostle who does not owe his authority to men or his appointment to any human being but who has been appointed by Jesus Christ and by God the Father who raised Jesus from the dead. ³We wish you the grace and peace of God our Father and of the Lord Jesus Christ, ⁴who in order to rescue us from this present wicked world sacrificed himself for our sins, in accordance with the will of God our Father, ⁵to whom be glory for ever and ever. Amen.

A warning

⁶I am astonished at the promptness with which you have turned away from the one who called you and have decided to follow a different version of the Good News. ⁷Not that there can be more than one Good News; it is merely that some troublemakers among you want to change the Good News of Christ; ⁸and let me warn you that if anyone

preaches a version of the Good News different from the one we have already preached to you, whether it be ourselves or an angel from heaven, he is to be condemned. [9]I am only repeating what we told you before: if anyone preaches a version of the Good News different from the one you have already heard, he is to be condemned. [10]So now whom am I trying to please - man, or God? Would you say it is men's approval I am looking for?[a] If I still wanted that, I should not be what I am - a servant of Christ.

I. PAUL'S APOLOGIA

God's call

[11]The fact is, brothers, and I want you to realise this, the Good News I preached is not a human message [12]that I was given by men, it is something I learnt only through a revelation of Jesus Christ. [13]You must have heard of my career as a practising Jew, how merciless I was in persecuting the Church of God, how much damage I did to it, [14]how I stood out among other Jews of my generation, and how enthusiastic I was for the traditions of my ancestors.

[15]Then God, who had specially *chosen* me while I was *still in my mother's womb,*[b] called me through his grace and chose [16]to reveal his Son in me, so that I

[1a]. Probably a rejoinder to an accusation by the judaisers that Paul was trying to make the pagans' conversion easy by not insisting on circumcision.   [1b]. Is 49:1.

might preach the Good News about him to the pagans. I did not stop to discuss this with any human being, [17]nor did I go up to Jerusalem to see those who were already apostles before me, but I went off to Arabia[c] at once and later went straight back from there to Damascus. [18]Even when after three years I went up to Jerusalem to visit Cephas and stayed with him for fifteen days, [19]I did not see any of the other apostles; I only saw James, the brother of the Lord, [20]and I swear before God that what I have just written is the literal truth. [21]After that I went to Syria and Cilicia, [22]and was still not known by sight to the churches of Christ in Judaea, [23]who had heard nothing except that their one-time persecutor was now preaching the faith he had previously tried to destroy; [24]and they gave glory to God for me.

The meeting at Jerusalem

2 [1]It was not till fourteen years had passed that I went up to Jerusalem again. I went with Barnabas and took Titus with me. [2]I went there as the result of a revelation, and privately I laid before the leading men the Good News as I proclaim it among the pagans; I did so for fear the course I was adopting or had already adopted would not be allowed. [3]And what happened?

[1c] Probably the kingdom of the Nabataean Arabs, to the S. of Damascus.

Even though Titus who had come with me is a Greek, he was not obliged to be circumcised. [4]The question came up only because some who do not really belong to the brotherhood have furtively crept in to spy on the liberty we enjoy in Christ Jesus, and want to reduce us all to slavery. [5]I was so determined to safeguard for you the true meaning of the Good News, that I refused even out of deference to yield to such people for one moment. [6]As a result, these people who are acknowledged leaders - not that their importance matters to me, since God has no favourites - these leaders, as I say, had nothing to add to the Good News as I preach it. [7]On the contrary, they recognised that I had been commissioned to preach the Good News to the uncircumcised just as Peter had been commissioned to preach it to the circumcised. [8]The same person whose action had made Peter the apostle of the circumcised had given me a similar mission to the pagans. [9]So, James, Cephas and John, these leaders, these pillars, shook hands with Barnabas and me as a sign of partnership: we were to go to the pagans and they to the circumcised.[a] [10]The only thing they insisted on was that we should remember to help the poor, as indeed I was anxious to do.

[2 a.] The distinction is geographical rather than racial; when Paul went among the Gentiles the resident Jews were his first concern.

Peter and Paul at Antioch

¹¹When Cephas came to Antioch, however, I opposed him to his face, since he was manifestly in the wrong. ¹²His custom had been to eat with the pagans,ᵇ but after certain friends of James arrived he stopped doing this and kept away from them altogether for fear of the group that insisted on circumcision. ¹³The other Jews joined him in this pretence, and even Barnabas felt himself obliged to copy their behaviour.

¹⁴When I saw they were not respecting the true meaning of the Good News, I said to Cephas in front of everyone, 'In spite of being a Jew, you live like the pagans and not like the Jews, so you have no right to make the pagans copy Jewish ways'.

The Good News as proclaimed by Paul

¹⁵'Though we were born Jews and not pagan sinners, ¹⁶we acknowledge that what makes a man righteous is not obedience to the Law, but faith in Jesus Christ. We had to become believers in Christ Jesus no less than you had, and now we hold that faith in Christ rather than fidelity to the Law is what justifies us, and that *no one can be justified*ᶜ by keeping the Law. ¹⁷Now if we were to admit that the result of looking to Christ to

---

²ᵇ Converts from paganism.   ²ᶜ Ps 143:2.

justify us is to make us sinners like the rest, it would follow that Christ had induced us to sin, which would be absurd. [18]If I were to return to a position I had already abandoned, I should be admitting I had done something wrong. [19]In other words, through the Law I am dead to the Law, so that now I can live for God. I have been crucified with Christ, [20]and I live now not with my own life but with the life of Christ who lives in me. The life I now live in this body I live in faith: faith in the Son of God who loved me and who sacrificed himself for my sake. [21]I cannot bring myself to give up God's gift: if the Law can justify us, there is no point in the death of Christ.'

II. DOCTRINAL MATTERS

Justification by faith

3 [1]Are you people in Galatia mad? Has someone put a spell on you, in spite of the plain explanation you have had of the crucifixion of Jesus Christ? [2]Let me ask you one question: was it because you practised the Law that you received the Spirit, or because you believed what was preached to you? [3]Are you foolish enough to end in outward observances what you began in the Spirit? [4]Have all the favours you received been wasted? And if this were so, they would most certainly have been wasted.

⁵Does God give you the Spirit so freely and work miracles among you because you practice Law, or because you believed what was preached to you?

⁶Take Abraham for example: *he put his faith in God, and this faith was considered as justifying him.*ᵃ ⁷Don't you see that it is those who rely on faith who are the sons of Abraham? ⁸Scripture foresaw that God was going to use faith to justify the pagans, and proclaimed the Good News long ago when Abraham was told: *In you all the pagans will be blessed.*ᵇ ⁹Those therefore who rely on faith receive the same blessing as Abraham, the man of faith.

The curse brought by the Law

¹⁰On the other hand, those who rely on the keeping of the Law are under a curse, since scripture says: *Cursed be everyone who does not persevere in observing everything prescribed in the book of the Law.*ᶜ ¹¹The Law will not justify anyone in the sight of God, because we are told: *the righteous man finds life through faith.*ᵈ ¹²The Law is not even based on faith, since we are told: *The man who practises these precepts finds life through practising them.*ᵉ ¹³Christ redeemed us from the curse of the Law by being cursed for our sake, since scripture says: *Cursed be everyone who is hanged on a tree.*ᶠ ¹⁴This was done so that

---

3 ᵃ. Gn 15:6.　3 ᵇ. Gn 12:3.　3 ᶜ. Dt 27:26.　3 ᵈ. Hab 2:4.　3 ᵉ. Lv 18:5.
3 ᶠ. Dt 21:23.

in Christ Jesus the blessing of Abraham might include the pagans, and so that through faith we might receive the promised Spirit.

The Law did not cancel the promise

[15]Compare this, brothers, with what happens in ordinary life. If a will has been drawn up in due form, no one is allowed to disregard it or add to it. [16]Now the promises were addressed to Abraham *and to his descendants* - notice, in passing, that scripture does not use a plural word as if there were several descendants, it uses the singular: to his posterity, which is Christ. [17]But my point is this: once God had expressed his will in due form, no law that came four hundred and thirty years later could cancel that and make the promise meaningless. [18]If you inherit something as a legal right, it does not come to you as the result of a promise, and it was precisely in the form of a promise that God made his gift to Abraham.

The purpose of the Law

[19]What then was the purpose of adding the Law? This was done to specify crimes, until the posterity came to whom the promise was addressed. The Law was promulgated by angels,[g] assisted by an intermediary.

[3 g.] In Jewish tradition angels were present at Sinai; the 'intermediary' is Moses.

²⁰Now there can only be an intermediary between two parties, yet God is one. ²¹Does this mean that there is opposition between the Law and the promises of God? Of course not. We could have been justified by the Law if the Law we were given had been capable of giving life, ²²but it is not: scripture makes no exceptions when it says that sin is master everywhere. In this way the promise can only be given through faith in Jesus Christ and can only be given to those who have this faith.

The coming of faith

²³Before faith came, we were allowed no freedom by the Law; we were being looked after till faith was revealed. ²⁴The Law was to be our guardian until the Christ came and we could be justified by faith. ²⁵Now that that time has come we are no longer under that guardian, ²⁶and you are, all of you, sons of God through faith in Christ Jesus. ²⁷All baptised in Christ, you have all clothed yourselves in Christ, ²⁸and there are no more distinctions between Jew and Greek, slave and free, male and female, but all of you are one in Christ Jesus. ²⁹Merely by belonging to Christ you are the posterity of Abraham, the heirs he was promised.

Sons of God

4 ¹Let me put this another way: an heir, even if he has actually inherited everything, is no different from a slave for as long as he remains a child. ²He is under the

control of guardians and administrators until he reaches the age fixed by his father. ³Now before we came of age we were as good as slaves to the elemental principles of this world,ᵃ ⁴but when the appointed time came, God sent his Son, born of a woman, born a subject of the Law, ⁵to redeem the subjects of the Law and to enable us to be adopted as sons. ⁶The proof that you are sons is that God has sent the Spirit of his Son into our hearts: the Spirit that cries, 'Abba, Father', ⁷and it is this that makes you a son, you are not a slave any more; and if God has made you son, then he has made you heir.

⁸Once you were ignorant of God, and enslaved to 'gods' who are not really gods at all; ⁹but now that you have come to acknowledge God - or rather, now that God has acknowledged you - how can you want to go back to elemental things like these, that can do nothing and give nothing, and be their slaves? ¹⁰You and your special days and months and seasons and years! ¹¹You make me feel I have wasted my time with you.

A personal appeal

¹²Brothers, all I ask is that you should copy me as I copied you. You have never treated me in an unfriendly way before; ¹³even at the beginning, when that illness

---

⁴ ᵃ. The principles that make up the physical universe; Paul has related the Law to 'outward observances', 3:3.

gave me the opportunity to preach the Good News to you, [14]you never showed the least sign of being revolted or disgusted by my disease that was such a trial to you; instead you welcomed me as an angel of God, as if I were Christ Jesus himself. [15]What has become of this enthusiasm you had? I swear that you would even have gone so far as to pluck out your eyes and give them to me. [16]Is it telling you the truth that has made me your enemy? [17]The blame lies in the way they have tried to win you over: by separating you from me, they want to win you over to themselves. [18]It is always a good thing to win people over - and I do not have to be there with you - but it must be for a good purpose, [19]my children! I must go through the pain of giving birth to you all over again, until Christ is formed in you. [20]I wish I were with you now so that I could know exactly what to say; as it is, I have no idea what to do for the best.

The two covenants: Hagar and Sarah

[21]You want to be subject to the Law? Then listen to what the Law says. [22]It says, if you remember, that Abraham had two sons, one by the slave-girl, and one by his free-born wife. [23]The child of the slave-girl was born in the ordinary way; the child of the free woman was born as the result of a promise. [24]This can be regarded as an allegory: the women stand for the two covenants. The first who comes from Mount Sinai, and whose children

are slaves, is Hagar - [25]since Sinai is in Arabia - and she corresponds to the present Jerusalem that is a slave like her children. [26]The Jerusalem above, however, is free and is our mother, since scripture says: *Shout for joy, you barren women who bore no children! Break into shouts of joy and gladness, you who were never in labour. For there are more sons of the forsaken one than sons of the wedded wife.*[b] [28]Now you, my brothers, like Isaac, are children of the promise, [29]and as at that time the child born in the ordinary way persecuted the child born in the Spirit's way, so also now. [30]Does not scripture say: *Drive away that slave-girl and her son; this slave-girl's son is not to share the inheritance with the son*[c] of the free woman? [31]So, my brothers, we are the children, not of the slave-girl, but of the free-born wife.

III. EXHORTATION

Christian liberty

5 [1]When Christ freed us, he meant us to remain free. Stand firm, therefore, and do not submit again to the yoke of slavery. [2]It is I, Paul, who tell you this: if you allow yourselves to be circumcised, Christ will be of no benefit to you at all. [3]With all solemnity I repeat my warning: Everyone who accepts circumcision is obliged

---

4 b. Is 54:1.   4 c. Gn 21:10.

to keep the whole Law. [4]But if you do look to the Law to make you justified, then you have separated yourselves from Christ, and have fallen from grace. [5]Christians are told by the Spirit to look to faith for those rewards that righteousness hopes for, [6]since in Christ Jesus whether you are circumcised or not makes no difference - what matters is faith that makes its power felt through love.

[7]You began your race well: who made you less anxious to obey the truth? [8]You were not prompted by him who called you! [9]The yeast seems to be spreading through the whole batch of you. [10]I feel sure that, united in the Lord, you will agree with me, and anybody who troubles you in future will be condemned, no matter who he is. [11]As for me, my brothers, if I still preach circumcision,[a] why am I still persecuted? If I did that now, would there be any scandal of the cross? [12]Tell those who are disturbing you I would like to see the knife slip.

Liberty and charity

[13]My brothers, you were called, as you know, to liberty; but be careful, or this liberty will provide an opening for self-indulgence. Serve one another, rather, in works of love, [14]since the whole of the Law is summarised in a single command: *Love your neighbour as yourself.*[b]

[5a] As Paul's enemies were apparently claiming.   [5b] Lv 19:18.

¹⁵If you go snapping at each other and tearing each other to pieces, you had better watch or you will destroy the whole community.

¹⁶Let me put it like this: if you are guided by the Spirit you will be in no danger of yielding to self-indulgence, ¹⁷since self-indulgence is the opposite of the Spirit, the Spirit is totally against such a thing, and it is precisely because the two are so opposed that you do not always carry out your good intentions. ¹⁸If you are led by the Spirit, no law can touch you. ¹⁹When self-indulgence is at work the results are obvious: fornication, gross indecency and sexual irresponsibility; ²⁰idolatry and sorcery; feuds and wrangling, jealousy, bad temper and quarrels; disagreements, factions, ²¹envy; drunkenness, orgies and similar things. I warn you now, as I warned you before: those who behave like this will not inherit the kingdom of God. ²²What the Spirit brings is very different: love, joy, peace, patience, kindness, goodness, trustfulness, ²³gentleness and self-control. There can be no law against things like that, of course. ²⁴You cannot belong to Christ Jesus unless you crucify all self-indulgent passions and desires.

²⁵Since the Spirit is our life, let us be directed by the Spirit. ²⁶We must stop being conceited, provocative and envious.

On kindness and perseverance

6 ¹Brothers, if one of you misbehaves, the more spiritual of you who set him right should do so in a spirit of gentleness, not forgetting that you may be tempted yourselves. ²You should carry each other's troubles and fulfil the law of Christ. ³It is the people who are not important who often make the mistake of thinking that they are. ⁴Let each of you examine his own conduct; if you find anything to boast about, it will at least be something of your own, not just something better than your neighbour has. ⁵Everyone has his own burden to carry.

⁶People under instruction should always contribute something to the support of the man who is instructing them.

⁷Don't delude yourself into thinking God can be cheated: where a man sows, there he reaps: ⁸if he sows in the field of self-indulgence he will get a harvest of corruption out of it; if he sows in the field of the Spirit he will get from it a harvest of eternal life. ⁹We must never get tired of doing good because if we don't give up the struggle we shall get our harvest at the proper time. ¹⁰While we have the chance, we must do good to all, and especially to our brothers in the faith.

Epilogue

[11]Take good note of what I am adding in my own handwriting and in large letters. [12]It is only self-interest that makes them want to force circumcision on you - they want to escape persecution for the cross of Christ - [13]they accept circumcision but do not keep the Law themselves; they only want you to be circumcised so that they can boast of the fact. [14]As for me, the only thing I can boast about is the cross of our Lord Jesus Christ, through whom the world is crucified to me, and I to the world. [15]It does not matter if a person is circumcised or not; what matters is for him to become an altogether new creature. [16]Peace and mercy to all who follow this rule, who form the Israel of God.

[17]I want no more trouble from anybody after this; the marks on my body are those of Jesus. [18]The grace of our Lord Jesus Christ be with your spirit, my brothers. Amen.

❧ EPHESIANS ❧

THE LETTER OF PAUL TO THE
CHURCH AT EPHESUS

Address and Greetings

1 ¹From Paul, appointed by God to be an apostle of Christ Jesus, to the saints who are faithful to Christ Jesus: ²Grace and peace to you from God our Father and from the Lord Jesus Christ.

I. THE MYSTERY OF SALVATION
AND OF THE CHURCH

God's plan of salvation

³Blessed be God the Father of our Lord Jesus Christ,
who has blessed us with all the spiritual blessings of
heaven in Christ.
⁴Before the world was made, he chose us, chose us
in Christ,
to be holy and spotless, and to live through love in
his presence,
⁵determining that we should become his adopted
sons, through Jesus Christ

for his own kind purposes,
[6]to make us praise the glory of his grace,
his free gift to us in the Beloved,
[7]in whom, through his blood, we gain our freedom,
     the forgiveness of our sins.
Such is the richness of the grace
[8]which he has showered on us
in all wisdom and insight.
[9]He has let us know the mystery of his purpose,
the hidden plan he so kindly made in Christ from
     the beginning
[10]to act upon when the times had run their course to
     the end:
that he would bring everything together under
     Christ, as head,
everything in the heavens and everything on earth.
[11]And it is in him that we were claimed as God's own,
chosen from the beginning,
under the predetermined plan of the one who guides
     all things
as he decides by his own will;
[12]chosen to be,
for his greater glory,
the people who would put their hopes in Christ
     before he came.
[13]Now you too, in him,
have heard the message of the truth and the good

news of your salvation,
and have believed it;
and you too have been stamped with the seal of the
Holy Spirit of the Promise,
[14]the pledge of our inheritance
which brings freedom for those whom God has
taken for his own,
to make his glory praised.

The triumph and the supremacy of Christ

[15]That will explain why I, having once heard about your faith in the Lord Jesus, and the love that you show towards all the saints, [16]have never failed to remember you in my prayers and to thank God for you. [17]May the God of our Lord Jesus Christ, the Father of glory, give you a spirit of wisdom and perception of what is revealed, to bring you to full knowledge of him. [18]May he enlighten the eyes of your mind so that you can see what hope his call holds for you, what rich glories he has promised the saints will inherit [19]and how infinitely great is the power that he has exercised for us believers. This you can tell from the strength of his power [20]at work in Christ, when he used it to raise him from the dead and to make him sit at his right hand, in heaven, [21]far above every Sovereignty, Authority, Power, or Domination,[a] or any other name that can be named not only in this age but

---

[1 a.] Orders of the angelic hierarchy in Jewish literature.

also in the age to come. ²²*He has put all things under his feet*,^b and made him, as the ruler of everything, the head of the Church; ²³which is his body, the fullness of him who fills the whole creation.

Salvation in Christ a free gift

2 ¹And you were dead, through the crimes and the sins ²in which you used to live when you were following the way of this world, obeying the ruler who governs the air,^a the spirit who is at work in the rebellious. ³We all were among them too in the past, living sensual lives, ruled entirely by our own physical desires and our own ideas; so that by nature we were as much under God's anger as the rest of the world. ⁴But God loved us with so much love that he was generous with his mercy: ⁵when we were dead through our sins, he brought us to life with Christ - it is through grace that you have been saved - ⁶and raised us up with him and gave us a place with him in heaven, in Christ Jesus.

⁷This was to show for all ages to come, through his goodness towards us in Christ Jesus, how infinitely rich he is in grace. ⁸Because it is by grace that you have been saved, through faith; not by anything of your own, but by a gift from God; ⁹not by anything that you have done,

---

[1] b. Ps 8:6.
[2] a. Satan.

so that nobody can claim the credit. [10]We are God's work of art, created in Christ Jesus to live the good life as from the beginning he had meant us to live it.

Reconciliation of the Jews and the pagans with each other and with God

[11]Do not forget, then, that there was a time when you who were pagans physically, termed the Uncircumcised by those who speak of themselves as the Circumcision by reason of a physical operation, [12]do not forget, I say, that you had no Christ and were excluded from membership of Israel, aliens with no part in the covenants with their Promise; you were immersed in this world, without hope and without God. [13]But now in Christ Jesus, you that used to be so far apart from us have been brought very close, by the blood of Christ. [14]For he is the peace between us, and has made the two into one and broken down the barrier which used to keep them apart, actually destroying in his own person the hostility [15]caused by the rules and decrees of the Law. This was to create one single New Man in himself out of the two of them and by restoring peace [16]through the cross, to unite them both in a single Body and reconcile them with God. In his own person he killed the hostility. [17]Later he came to bring the good news of peace, *peace to you who were far away and peace to those who were near*

at hand.[b] [18]Through him, both of us have in the one
Spirit our way to come to the Father.

[19]So you are no longer aliens or foreign visitors: you
are citizens like all the saints, and part of God's
household. [20]You are part of a building that has the
apostles and prophets[c] for its foundations, and Christ
Jesus himself for its main cornerstone. [21]As every
structure is aligned on him, all grow into one holy temple
in the Lord; [22]and you too, in him, are being built into a
house where God lives, in the Spirit.

Paul, a servant of the mystery

3 [1]So I, Paul, a prisoner of Christ Jesus for the sake of you
pagans... [2]You have probably heard how I have been
entrusted by God with the grace he meant for you, [3]and that
it was by a revelation that I was given the knowledge of the
mystery, as I have just described it very shortly. [4]If you read
my word you will have some idea of the depths that I see in
the mystery of Christ. [5]This that has now been revealed
through the Spirit to his holy apostles and prophets was
unknown to any men in past generations; [6]it means that
pagans now share the same inheritance, that they are parts
of the same body, and that the same promise has been made
to them, in Jesus Christ, through the gospel. [7]I have been
made the servant of that gospel by a gift of grace from God

[2b] Is 57:19. [2c] The N.T. prophets.

who gave it to me by his own power. [8]I, who am less than the least of all the saints, have been entrusted with this special grace, not only of proclaiming to the pagans the infinite treasure of Christ [9]but also of explaining how the mystery is to be dispensed. Through all the ages, this has been kept hidden in God, the creator of everything. Why? [10]So that the Sovereignties and Powers should learn only now, through the Church, how comprehensive God's wisdom really is, [11]exactly according to the plan which he had had from all eternity in Christ Jesus our Lord. [12]This is why we are bold enough to approach God in complete confidence, through our faith in him; [13]so, I beg you, never lose confidence just because of the trials that I go through on your account: they are your glory.

Paul's prayer

[14]This, then, is what I pray, kneeling before the Father, [15]from whom every family,[a] whether spiritual or natural, takes its name:

[16]Out of his infinite glory, may he give you the power through his Spirit for your hidden self to grow strong, [17]so that Christ may live in your hearts through faith, and then, planted in love and built on love, [18]you will with all the saints have strength to grasp the breadth and the length,

---

[3][a.] A pun on the words 'Father' and 'family' (clan or tribe) is lost in translation; traces of it survive in *paternity* and *patriotism*.

the height and the depth; [19]until, knowing the love of Christ, which is beyond all knowledge, you are filled with the utter fullness of God.

[20]Glory be to him whose power, working in us, can do infinitely more than we can ask or imagine; [21]glory be to him from generation to generation in the Church and in Christ Jesus for ever and ever. Amen.

II. EXHORTATION

A call to unity

4 [1]I, the prisoner in the Lord, implore you therefore to lead a life worthy of your vocation. [2]Bear with one another charitably, in complete selflessness, gentleness and patience. [3]Do all you can to preserve the unity of the Spirit by the peace that binds you together. [4]There is one Body, one Spirit, just as you were all called into one and the same hope when you were called. [5]There is one Lord, one faith, one baptism, [6]and one God who is Father of all, over all, through all and within all.

[7]Each one of us, however, has been given his own share of grace, given as Christ allotted it. [8]It was said that he would:

When he ascended to the height, he captured
    prisoners,
  he gave gifts to men.[a]

[4a]. Ps 68:18.

⁹When it says, 'he ascended', what can it mean if not that he descended right down to the lower regions of the earth? ¹⁰The one who rose higher than all the heavens to fill all things is none other than the one who descended. ¹¹And to some, his gift was that they should be apostles; to some, prophets; to some, evangelists; to some, pastors and teachers; ¹²so that the saints together make a unity in the work of service, building up the body of Christ. ¹³In this way we are all to come to unity in our faith and in our knowledge of the Son of God, until we become the perfect Man, fully mature with the fullness of Christ himself.

¹⁴Then we shall not be children any longer, or tossed one way and another and carried along by every wind of doctrine, at the mercy of all the tricks men play and their cleverness in practising deceit. ¹⁵If we live by the truth and in love, we shall grow in all ways into Christ, who is the head ¹⁶by whom the whole body is fitted and joined together, every joint adding its own strength, for each separate part to work according to its function. So the body grows until it has built itself up, in love.

The new life in Christ

¹⁷In particular, I want to urge you in the name of the Lord, not to go on living the aimless kind of life that pagans live. ¹⁸Intellectually they are in the dark, and they are estranged from the life of God, without knowledge because

they have shut their hearts to it. [19]Their sense of right and wrong once dulled, they have abandoned themselves to sexuality and eagerly pursue a career of indecency of every kind. [20]Now that is hardly the way you have learnt from Christ, [21]unless you failed to hear him properly when you were taught what the truth is in Jesus. [22]You must give up your old way of life; you must put aside your old self, which gets corrupted by following illusory desires. [23]Your mind must be renewed by a spiritual revolution [24]so that you can put on the new self that has been created in God's way, in the goodness and holiness of the truth.

[25]So from now on, there must be no more lies: *You must speak the truth to one another,*[b] since we are all parts of one another. [26]*Even if you are angry, you must not sin:*[c] never let the sun set on your anger [27]or else you will give the devil a foothold. [28]Anyone who was a thief must stop stealing; he should try to find some useful manual work instead, and be able to do some good by helping others that are in need. [29]Guard against foul talk; let your words be for the improvement of others, as occasion offers, and do good to your listeners, [30]otherwise you will only be grieving the Holy Spirit of God who has marked you with his seal for you to be set free when the day comes. [31]Never have grudges against others, or lose your temper, or raise your voice to anybody, or call each other names,

---

[4]b. Zc 8:16. [4]c. Ps 4:4 (LXX).

or allow any sort of spitefulness. [32]Be friends with one another, and kind, forgiving each other as readily as God forgave you in Christ.

5 [1]Try, then, to imitate God as children of his that he loves, [2]and follow Christ loving as he loved you, giving himself up in our place *as a fragrant offering and a sacrifice to God*.[a] [3]Among you there must be not even a mention of fornication or impurity in any of its forms, or promiscuity: this would hardly become the saints! [4]There must be no coarseness, or salacious talk and jokes - all this is wrong for you; raise your voices in thanksgiving instead. [5]For you can be quite certain that nobody who actually indulges in fornication or impurity or promiscuity - which is worshipping a false god - can inherit anything of the kingdom of God. [6]Do not let anyone deceive you with empty arguments: it is for this loose living that God's anger comes down on those who rebel against him. [7]Make sure that you are not included with them. [8]You were darkness once, but now you are light in the Lord; be like children of light, [9]for the effects of the light are seen in complete goodness and right living and truth. [10]Try to discover what the Lord wants of you, [11]having nothing to do with the futile works of darkness but exposing them by contrast. [12]The things which are done in secret are

---

[5a] Ex 29:18.

things that ashamed even to speak of; [13]but anything exposed by the light will be illuminated [14]and anything illuminated turns into light. That is why it is said:[b]

> Wake up from your sleep,
> rise from the dead,
> and Christ will shine on you.

[15]So be very careful about the sort of lives you lead, like intelligent and not like senseless people. [16]This may be a wicked age, but you redeem it. [17]And do not be thoughtless but recognise what is the will of the Lord. [18]Do not drug yourselves with wine, this is simply dissipation; be filled with the Spirit. [19]Sing the words and tunes of the psalms and hymns when you are together, and go on singing and chanting to the Lord in your hearts, [20]so that always and everywhere you are giving thanks to God who is our Father in the name of our Lord Jesus Christ.

The morals of the home

[21]Give way to one another in obedience to Christ. [22]Wives should regard their husbands as they regard the Lord, [23]since as Christ is head of the Church and saves the whole body, so is a husband the head of his wife; [24]and as the Church submits to Christ, so should wives to their husbands, in everything. [25]Husbands should love their

---

[5 b.] Presumably a quotation from a Christian hymn.

wives just as Christ loved the Church and sacrificed himself for her [26]to make her holy. He made her clean by washing her in water with a form of words, [27]so that when he took her to himself she would be glorious, with no speck or wrinkle or anything like that, but holy and faultless. [28]In the same way, husbands must love their wives as they love their own bodies; for a man to love his wife is for him to love himself. [29]A man never hates his own body, but he feeds it and looks after it; and that is the way Christ treats the Church, [30]because it is his body - and we are its living parts. [31]*For this reason, a man must leave his father and mother and be joined to his wife, and the two will become one body.*[c] [32]This mystery has many implications; but I am saying it applies to Christ and the Church. [33]To sum up; you too, each one of you, must love his wife as he loves himself; and let every wife respect her husband.

6 [1]Children, be obedient to your parents in the Lord - that is your duty. [2]The commandment that has a promise attached to it is: *Honour your father and mother,* [3]and the promise is: *and you will prosper and have a long life in the land.*[a] [4]And parents, never drive your children to resentment but in bringing them up correct them and guide them as the Lord does.

[5c.] Gn 2:24.
[6a.] Ex 20:12.

⁵Slaves, be obedient to the men who are called your masters in this world, with deep respect and sincere loyalty, as you are obedient to Christ: ⁶not only when you are under their eye, as if you had only to please men, but because you are slaves of Christ and wholeheartedly do the will of God. ⁷Work hard and willingly, but do it for the sake of the Lord and not for the sake of men. ⁸You can be sure that everyone, whether a slave or a free man, will be properly rewarded by the Lord for whatever work he has done well. ⁹And those of you who are employers, treat your slaves in the same spirit; do without threats, remembering that they and you have the same Master in heaven and he is not impressed by one person more than by another.

The spiritual war

¹⁰Finally, grow strong in the Lord, with the strength of his power. ¹¹Put God's armour on so as to be able to resist the devil's tactics. ¹²For it is not against human enemies that we have to struggle, but against the Sovereignties and the Powers who originate the darkness in this world, the spiritual army of evil in the heavens. ¹³That is why you must rely on God's armour, or you will not be able to put up any resistance when the worst happens, or have enough resources to hold your ground.

[14]So stand your ground, with *truth buckled round your waist*, and *integrity for a breastplate*,[b] [15]wearing for shoes on your feet *the eagerness to spread the gospel of peace*[c] [16]and always carrying the shield of faith so that you can use it to put out the burning arrows of the evil one. [17]And then you must accept *salvation from God to be your helmet* and receive the word of God from the Spirit to use as a sword.

[18]Pray all the time, asking for what you need, praying in the Spirit on every possible occasion. Never get tired of staying awake to pray for all the saints; [19]and pray for me to be given an opportunity to open my mouth and speak without fear and give out the mystery of the gospel [20]of which I am an ambassador in chains; pray that in proclaiming it I may speak as boldly as I ought to.

Personal news and final salutation

[21]I should like you to know, as well, what is happening to me and what I am doing; my dear brother Tychicus, my loyal helper in the Lord, will tell you everything. [22]I am sending him to you precisely for this purpose, to give you news about us and reassure you.

[23]May God the Father and the Lord Jesus Christ grant peace, love and faith to all the brothers. [24]May grace and eternal life be with all who love our Lord Jesus Christ.

[6b.] Is 59:17.   [6c.] Is 40:9.

❧ PHILIPPIANS ❧

THE LETTER OF PAUL TO THE
CHURCH AT PHILIPPI

Address

1 ¹From Paul and Timothy, servants of Christ Jesus, to all the saints in Christ Jesus, together with their presiding elders and deacons.[a] ²We wish you the grace and peace of God our Father and of the Lord Jesus Christ.

Thanksgiving and prayer

³I thank my God whenever I think of you; and ⁴every time I pray for all of you, I pray with joy, ⁵remembering how you have helped to spread the Good News from the day you first heard it right up to the present. ⁶I am quite certain that the One who began this good work in you will see that it is finished when the Day of Christ Jesus comes. ⁷It is only natural that I should feel like this towards you all, since you have shared the privileges which have been mine: both my chains and my work defending and establishing the gospel. You have a permanent place in my heart, ⁸and God knows

---

¹ a. Jb 13:16 (LXX).

how much I miss you all, loving you as Christ Jesus loves you. [9]My prayer is that your love for each other may increase more and more and never stop improving your knowledge and deepening your perception. [10]so that you can always recognise what is best. This will help you to become pure and blameless, and prepare you for the Day of Christ, [11]when you will reach the perfect goodness which Jesus Christ produces in us for the glory and praise of God.

Paul's own circumstances

[12]I am glad to tell you, brothers, that the things that happened to me have actually been a help to the Good News.

[13]My chains, in Christ, have become famous not only all over the Praetorium but everywhere, [14]and most of the brothers have taken courage in the Lord from these chains of mine and are getting more and more daring in announcing the Message without any fear. [15]It is true that some of them are doing it just out of rivalry and competition, but the rest preach Christ with the right intention, [16]out of nothing but love, as they know that this is my invariable way of defending the gospel. [17]The others, who proclaim Christ for jealous or selfish motives, do not mind if they make my chains heavier to bear. [18]But does it matter? Whether from dishonest motives or in sincerity, Christ is proclaimed; and that makes me happy; [19]and I shall continue being happy, because I know *this will help to save me*, thanks to your prayers and to the

help which will be given to me by the Spirit of Jesus. [20]My one hope and trust is that I shall never have to admit defeat, but that now as always I shall have the courage for Christ to be glorified in my body, whether by my life or by my death. [21]Life to me, of course, is Christ, but then death would bring me something more; [22]but then again, if living in this body means doing work which is having good results - I do not know what I should choose. [23]I am caught in this dilemma: I want to be gone and be with Christ, which would be very much the better, [24]but for me to stay alive in this body is a more urgent need for your sake. [25]This weighs with me so much that I feel sure I shall survive and stay with you all, and help you to progress in the faith and even increase your joy in it; [26]and so you will have another reason to give praise to Christ Jesus on my account when I am with you again.

Fight for the faith

[27]Avoid anything in your everyday lives that would be unworthy of the gospel of Christ, so that, whether I come to you and see for myself, or stay at a distance and only hear about you, I shall know that you are unanimous in meeting the attack with firm resistance, united by your love for the faith of the gospel [28]and quite unshaken by your enemies. This would be the sure sign that they will lose and you will be saved. It would be a sign from God [29]that he has given you the privilege not only of believing

in Christ, but of suffering for him as well. [30]You and I are together in the same fight as you saw me fighting before and, as you will have heard, I am fighting still.

Preserve unity in humility

2 [1]If our life in Christ means anything to you, if love can persuade at all, or the Spirit that we have in common, or any tenderness and sympathy, [2]then be united in your convictions and united in your love, with a common purpose and a common mind. That is the one thing which would make me completely happy. [3]There must be no competition among you, no conceit; but everybody is to be self-effacing. Always consider the other person to be better than yourself, [4]so that nobody thinks of his own interests first but everybody thinks of other s people's interests instead. [5]In your minds you must be the same as Christ Jesus:[a]

> [6]His state was divine,
> yet he did not cling
> to his equality with God
> [7]but emptied himself
> to assume the condition of a slave,
> and became as men are;
> and being as all men are,

---

[2][a]. Vv. 6.11 are a hymn, though whether composed or only quoted by Paul is uncertain.

[8]he was humbler yet,
even to accepting death,
death on a cross.
[9]But God raised him high
and gave him the name
which is above all other names
[10]so that *all beings*
in the heavens, on earth and in the underworld,
should bend the knee[b] at the name of Jesus
[11]and that every tongue should acclaim
Jesus Christ as Lord,
to the glory of God the Father.

Work for salvation

[12]So then, my dear friends, continue to do as I tell you, as you always have; not only as you did when I was there with you, but even more now that I am no longer there; and work for your salvation 'in fear and trembling'. [13]It is God, for his own loving purpose, who puts both the will and the action into you. [14]Do all that has to be done without complaining or arguing [15]and then you will be innocent and genuine, *perfect children of God among a deceitful and underhand brood,*[c] and you will shine in the world like bright stars [16]because you are offering it the word of life. This would give me something to be proud

---

[2b] Is 45:23.   [2c] Dt 32:5.

of for the Day of Christ, and would mean that I had not run in the race and exhausted myself for nothing. ¹⁷And then, if my blood has to be shed as part of your own sacrifice and offering - which is your faith^d - I shall still be happy and rejoice with all of you, ¹⁸and you must be just as happy and rejoice with me.

The mission of Timothy and Epaphroditus

¹⁹I hope, in the Lord Jesus, to send Timothy to you soon, and I shall be reassured by having news of you. ²⁰I have nobody else like him here, as wholeheartedly concerned for your welfare: ²¹all the rest seem more interested in themselves than in Jesus Christ. ²²But you know how he has proved himself by working with me on behalf of the Good News like a son helping his father. ²³That is why he is the one that I am hoping to send you, as soon as I know something definite about my fate. ²⁴But I continue to trust, in the Lord, that I shall be coming soon myself.

²⁵It is essential, I think, to send brother Epaphroditus back to you. He was sent as your representative to help me when I needed someone to be my companion in working and battling, ²⁶but he misses you all and is worried because you heard about his illness. ²⁷It is true that he has been ill, and almost died, but God took pity on

---

^{2 d.} Libations were common to Greek and Jewish sacrifices.

him, and on me as well as him, and spared me what would have been one grief on top of another. [28]So I shall send him back as promptly as I can; you will be happy to see him again, and that will make me less sorry. [29]Give him a most hearty welcome, in the Lord; people like him are to be honoured. [30]It was for Christ's work that he came so near to dying, and he risked his life to give me the help that you were not able to give me yourselves.

3 [1]Finally, my brothers, rejoice in the Lord.[a]

The true way of Christian salvation

It is no trouble to me to repeat what I have already written to you, and as far as you are concerned, it will make for safety. [2]Beware of dogs! Watch out for the people who are making mischief. Watch out for the cutters.[b] [3]We are the real people of the circumcision, we who worship in accordance with the Spirit of God; we have our own glory from Christ Jesus without having to rely on a physical operation. [4]If it came to relying on physical evidence, I should be fully qualified myself. Take any man who thinks he can rely on what is physical: I am even better qualified. [5]I was born of the race of Israel

---

[3a.] Paul's conclusion is interrupted by a long postscript.

[3b.] A contemptuous reference to the circumcisers comparing circumcision with self-inflicted gashes in pagan cults.

and of the tribe of Benjamin, a Hebrew born of Hebrew parents, and I was circumcised when I was eight days old. As for the Law, I was a Pharisee; [6]as for working for religion, I was a persecutor of the Church; as far as the Law can make you perfect, I was faultless. [7]But because of Christ, I have come to consider all these advantages that I had as disadvantages. [8]Not only that, but I believe nothing can happen that will outweigh the supreme advantage of knowing Christ Jesus my Lord. For him I have accepted the loss of everything, and I look on everything as so much rubbish if only I can have Christ [9]and be given a place in him. I am no longer trying for perfection by my own efforts, the perfection that comes from the Law, but I want only the perfection that comes through faith in Christ, and is from God and based on faith. [10]All I want is to know Christ and the power of his resurrection and to share his sufferings by reproducing the pattern of his death. [11]That is the way I can hope to take my place in the resurrection of the dead. [12]Not that I have become perfect yet: I have not yet won, but I am still running, trying to capture the prize for which Christ Jesus captured me. [13]I can assure you my brothers, I am far from thinking that I have already won. All I can say is that I forget the past and I strain ahead for what is still to come; [14]I am racing for the finish, for is the prize to which God calls us upwards to receive in Christ Jesus. [15]We who are called 'perfect' must all think in this way. If there is some point on which you see things differently, God will make it clear to you; [16]meanwhile, let us go forward on the road that has brought us to where we are.

[17]My brothers, be united in following my rule of life. Take as your models everybody who is already doing this and study them as you used to study us. [18]I have told you often, and I repeat it today with tears, there are many who are behaving as the enemies of the cross of Christ. [19]They are destined to be lost. They make foods into their god and they are proudest of something they ought to think shameful; the things they think important are earthly things. [20]For us, our homeland is in heaven, and from heaven comes the saviour we are waiting for, the Lord Jesus Christ, [21]and he will transfigure these wretched bodies of ours into copies of his glorious body. He will do that by the same power with which he can subdue the whole universe.

4 [1]So then, my brothers and dear friends, do not give way but remain faithful in the Lord. I miss you very much, dear friends; you are my joy and my crown.

Last advice

[2]I appeal to Evodia and I appeal to Syntyche to come to agreement with each other, in the Lord; [3]and I ask you, Syzygus,[a] to be truly a 'companion' and to help them in

---

[4a.] 'Companion' is the meaning of the proper name Syzygus.

this. These women were a help to me when I was fighting to defend the Good News - and so, at the same time, were Clement and the others who worked with me. Their names are written in the book of life.

⁴I want you to be happy, always happy in the Lord; I repeat, what I want is your happiness. ⁵Let your tolerance be evident to everyone: the Lord is very near. ⁶There is no need to worry; but if there is anything you need, pray for it, asking God for it with prayer and thanksgiving, ⁷and that peace of God, which is so much greater than we can understand, will guard your hearts and your thoughts, in Christ Jesus. ⁸Finally, brothers, fill your minds with everything that is true, everything that is noble, everything that is good and pure, everything that we love and honour, and everything that can be thought virtuous or worthy of praise. ⁹Keep doing all the things that you learnt from me and have been taught by me and have heard or seen that I do. Then the God of peace will be with you.

Thanks for help received

¹⁰It is a great joy to me, in the Lord, that at last you have shown some concern for me again; though of course you were concerned before, and only lacked an opportunity. ¹¹I am not talking about shortage of money: I have learnt to manage on whatever I have, ¹²I know how to be poor and I know how to be rich too. I have been

through my initiation and now I am ready for anything anywhere: full stomach or empty stomach, poverty or plenty. [13]There is nothing I cannot master with the help of the One who gives me strength. [14]All the same, it was good of you to share with me in my hardships. [15]In the early days of the Good News, as you people of Philippi well know, when I left Macedonia, no other church helped me with gifts of money. You were the only ones; [16]and twice since my stay in Thessalonika you have sent me what I needed. [17]It is not your gift that I value; what is valuable to me is the interest that is mounting up in your account. [18]Now for the time being I have everything that I need and more: I am fully provided now that I have received from Epaphroditus the offering that you sent, a *sweet fragrance* - the sacrifice that God accepts and finds pleasing. [19]In return my God will fulfil all your needs, in Christ Jesus, as lavishly as only God can. [20]Glory to God, our Father, for ever and ever. Amen.

Greetings and final wish

[21]My greetings to every one of the saints in Christ Jesus. The brothers who are with me send their greetings. [22]All the saints send their greetings, especially those of the imperial household.[b] [23]May the grace of the Lord Jesus Christ be with your spirit.

[4b.] I.e. in the service of the emperor.

❧ COLOSSIANS ❧

THE LETTER OF PAUL TO THE
CHURCH AT COLOSSAE

PREFACE

Address

1 ¹From Paul, appointed by God to be an apostle of
Christ Jesus, and from our brother Timothy ²to the
saints in Colossae, our faithful brothers in Christ: Grace
and peace to you from God our Father.

Thanksgiving and prayer

³We have never failed to remember you in our prayers and
to give thanks for you to God, the Father of our Lord Jesus
Christ, ⁴ever since we heard about your faith in Christ Jesus
and the love that you show towards all the saints ⁵because of
the hope which is stored up for you in heaven. It is only
recently that you heard of this, when it was announced in the
message of the truth. The Good News ⁶which has reached
you is spreading all over the world and producing the same
results as it has among you ever since the day when you
heard about God's grace and understood what this really is.
⁷Epaphras, who taught you, is one of our closest fellow

workers and a faithful deputy for us as Christ's servant, [8]and it was he who told us all about your love in the Spirit.

[9]That will explain why, ever since the day he told us, we have never failed to pray for you, and what we ask God is that through perfect wisdom and spiritual understanding you should reach the fullest knowledge of his will. [10]So you will be able to lead the kind of life which the Lord expects of you, a life acceptable to him in all its aspects; showing the results in all the good actions you do and increasing your knowledge of God. [11]You will have in you the strength, based on his own glorious power, never to give in, but to bear anything joyfully, [12]thanking the Father who has made it possible for you to join the saints and with them to inherit the light.

[13]Because that is what he has done: he has taken us out of the power of darkness and created a place for us in the kingdom of the Son that he loves, [14]and in him, we gain our freedom, the forgiveness of our sins.

I. FORMAL INSTRUCTION

Christ is the head of all creation

[15]He is the image of the unseen God
and the first-born of all creation,
[16]for in him were created
all things in heaven and on earth:
everything visible and everything invisible,
Thrones, Dominations, Sovereignties, Powers -

all things were created through him and for him.
[17]Before anything was created, he existed,
and he holds all things in unity.
Now the Church is his body,
he is its head.

[18]As he is the Beginning,
he was first to be born from the dead,
so that he should be first in every way;
[19]because God wanted all perfection
to be found in him
[20]and all things to be reconciled through him and
for him,
everything in heaven and everything on earth,
when he made peace
by his death on the cross.

The Colossians have their share in salvation

[21]Not long ago, you were foreigners and enemies, in the way that you used to think and the evil things that you did; [22]but now he has reconciled you, by his death and in that mortal body. Now you are able to appear before him holy, pure and blameless - [23]as long as you persevere and stand firm on the solid base of the faith, never letting yourselves drift away from the hope promised by the Good News, which you have heard, which has been preached to the whole human race, and of which I, Paul, have become the servant.

Paul's labours in the service of the pagans

[24]It makes me happy to suffer for you, as I am suffering now, and in my own body to do what I can to make up all that has still to be undergone by Christ for the sake of his body, the Church. [25]I became the servant of the Church when God made me responsible for delivering God's message to you, [26]the message which was a mystery hidden for generations and centuries and has now been revealed to his saints. [27]It was God's purpose to reveal it to them and to show all the rich glory of this mystery to pagans. The mystery is Christ among you, your hope of glory: [28]this is the Christ we proclaim, this is the wisdom in which we thoroughly train everyone and instruct everyone, to make them all perfect in Christ. [29]It is for this I struggle wearily on, helped only by his power driving me irresistibly.

Paul's concern for the Colossians' faith

2 [1]Yes, I want you to know that I do have to struggle hard for you, and for those in Laodicea, and for so many others who have never seen me face to face. [2]It is all to bind you together in love and to stir your minds, so that your understanding may come to full development, until you really know God's secret [3]in which all the jewels of wisdom and knowledge are hidden.

[4]I say this to make sure that no one deceives you with specious arguments. [5]I may be absent in body, but in spirit I am there among you, delighted to find you all in harmony and to see how firm your faith in Christ is.

II. A WARNING AGAINST SOME ERRORS

Live according to the true faith in Christ, not according to false teaching

[6]You must live your whole life according to the Christ you have received - Jesus the Lord; [7]you must be rooted in him and built on him and held firm by the faith you have been taught, and full of thanksgiving.

[8]Make sure that no one traps you and deprives you of your freedom by some secondhand, empty, rational philosophy based on the principles of this world instead of on Christ.

Christ alone is the true head of men and angels

[9]In his body lives the fullness of divinity, and in him you too find your own fulfilment, [10]in the one who is the head of every Sovereignty and Power.[a]

[11]In him you have been circumcised, with a circumcision not performed by human hand, but by the complete stripping of your body of flesh. This is

---

[a] i.e. over the highest orders of angels.

circumcision according to Christ. [12]You have been buried with him, when you were baptised; and by baptism, too, you have been raised up with him through your belief in the power of God who raised him from the dead. [13]You were dead, because you were sinners and had not been circumcised: he[b] has brought you to life with him, he has forgiven us all our sins.

[14]He has overridden the Law, and cancelled every record of the debt that we had to pay; he has done away with it by nailing it to the cross;[c] [15]and so he got rid of the Sovereignties and the Powers, and paraded them in public, behind him in his triumphal procession.[d]

Against the false asceticism based on 'the principles of this world'

[16]From now onwards, never let anyone else decide what you should eat or drink, or whether you are to observe annual festivals, New Moons or sabbaths. [17]These were only pale reflections of what was coming: the reality is Christ. [18]Do not be taken in by people who like grovelling to angels and worshipping them; people like that are always going on about some vision they have had, inflating themselves to a false importance with their worldly outlook. [19]A man of this sort is not united to the head, and

---

[2 b.] God the Father.   [2 c.] Destroying our death warrant.   [2 d.] The tradition was that the Law was brought down to Moses by angels.

it is the head that adds strength and holds the whole body together, with all its joints and sinews - and this is the only way in which it can reach its full growth in God.

²⁰If you have really died with Christ to the principles of this world, why do you still let rules dictate to you, as though you were still living in the world? ²¹'It is forbidden to pick up this, it is forbidden to taste that, it is forbidden to touch something else'; ²²all these prohibitions are only concerned with things that perish by their very use - an example of *human doctrines and regulations*!ᵉ ²³It may be argued that true wisdom is to be found in these, with their self-imposed devotions, their self-abasement, and their severe treatment of the body; but once the flesh starts to protest, they are no use at all.

Life-giving union with the glorified Christ

3 ¹Since you have been brought back to true life with Christ, you must look for the things that are in heaven, where Christ is, sitting at God's right hand. ²Let your thoughts be on heavenly things, not on the things that are on the earth, ³because you have died, and now the life you have is hidden with Christ in God. ⁴But when Christ is revealed - and he is your life - you too will be revealed in all your glory with him.

---

2 e. Is 29:13.

III. EXHORTATION

General rules of Christian behaviour

[5]That is why you must kill everything in you that belongs only to earthly life: fornication, impurity, guilty passion, evil desires and especially greed, which is the same thing as worshipping a false god; [6]all this is the sort of behaviour that makes God angry. [7]And it is the way in which you used to live when you were surrounded by people doing the same thing, [8]but now you, of all people, must give all these things up: getting angry, being bad-tempered, spitefulness, abusive language and dirty talk; [9]and never tell each other lies. You have stripped off your old behaviour with your old self, [10]and you have put on a new self which will progress towards true knowledge the more it is renewed in the image of its creator; [11]and in that image there is no room for distinction between Greek and Jew, between the circumcised or the uncircumcised, or between barbarian and Scythian, slave and free man. There is only Christ: he is everything and he is in everything.

[12]You are God's chosen race, his saints; he loves you, and you should be clothed in sincere compassion, in kindness and humility, gentleness and patience. [13]Bear with one another; forgive each other as soon as a quarrel begins. The Lord has forgiven you; now you

must do the same. [14]Over all these clothes, to keep them together and complete them, put on love. [15]And may the peace of Christ reign in your hearts, because it is for this that you were called together as parts of one body. Always be thankful.

[16]Let the message of Christ, in all its richness, find a home with you. Teach each other, and advise each other, in all wisdom. With gratitude in your hearts sing psalms and hymns and inspired songs to God; [17]and never say or do anything except in the name of the Lord Jesus, giving thanks to God the Father through him.

The morals of the home and household

[18]Wives, give way to your husbands, as you should in the Lord. [19]Husbands, love your wives and treat them with gentleness. [20]Children, be obedient to your parents always, because that is what will please the Lord. [21]Parents, never drive your children to resentment or you will make them feel frustrated.

[22]Slaves, be obedient to the men who are called your masters in this world; not only when you are under their eye, as if you had only to please men, but wholeheartedly, out of respect for the Master. [23]Whatever your work is, put your heart into it as if it were for the Lord and not for men, [24]knowing that the Lord will repay you by making you his heirs. It is Christ the Lord that you are serving;

²⁵anyone who does wrong will be repaid in kind and he does not favour one person more than another. **4** ¹Masters, make sure that your slaves are given what is just and fair, knowing that you too have a Master in heaven.

The apostolic spirit

²Be persevering in your prayers and be thankful as you stay awake to pray. ³Pray for us especially, asking God to show us opportunities for announcing the message and proclaiming the mystery of Christ, for the sake of which I am in chains; ⁴pray that I may proclaim it as clearly as I ought.

⁵Be tactful with those who are not Christians and be sure you make the best use of your time with them. ⁶Talk to them agreeably and with a flavour of wit, and try to fit your answers to the needs of each one.

Personal news

⁷Tychicus will tell you all the news about me. He is a brother I love very much, and a loyal helper and companion in the service of the Lord. ⁸I am sending him to you precisely for this purpose: to give you news about us and to reassure you. ⁹With him I am sending Onesimus, that dear and faithful brother who is a fellow citizen of yours. They will tell you everything that is happening here.

Greetings and final wishes

[10]Aristarchus, who is here in prison with me, sends his greetings, and so does Mark, the cousin of Barnabas - you were sent some instructions about him; if he comes to you give him a warm welcome. - [11]and Jesus Justus adds his greetings. Of all those who have come over from the Circumcision, these are the only ones actually working with me for the kingdom of God. They have been a great comfort to me. [12]Epaphras, your fellow citizen, sends his greetings; this servant of Christ Jesus never stops battling for you, praying that you will never lapse but always hold perfectly and securely to the will of God. [13]I can testify for him that he works hard for you, as well as for those at Laodicea and Hierapolis. [14]Greetings from my dear friend Luke, the doctor, and also from Demas.

[15]Please give my greetings to the brothers at Laodicea and to Nympha and the church which meets in her house. [16]After this letter has been read among you, send it on to be read in the church of the Laodiceans; and get the letter from Laodicea for you to read yourselves. [17]Give Archippus this message, 'Remember the service that the Lord wants you to do, and try to carry it out'.

[18]Here is a greeting in my own handwriting - PAUL. Remember the chains I wear. Grace be with you.

❧ 1 THESSALONIANS ❧

THE FIRST LETTER OF PAUL TO THE CHURCH
IN THESSALONIKA

Address

1 ¹From Paul, Silvanus and Timothy, to the Church in Thessalonika which is in God the Father and the Lord Jesus Christ; wishing you grace and peace.

Thanksgiving and congratulations

²We always mention you in our prayers and thank God for you all, ³and constantly remember before God our Father how you have shown your faith in action, worked for love and persevered through hope, in our Lord Jesus Christ.

⁴We know, brothers, that God loves you and that you have been chosen, ⁵because when we brought the Good News to you, it came to you not only as words, but as power and as the Holy Spirit and as utter conviction. And you observed the sort of life we lived when we were with you, which was for your instruction, ⁶and you were led to become imitators of us, and of the Lord; and it was with the joy of the Holy Spirit that you took to the gospel, in spite of the great opposition all round you. ⁷This has made you the great

example to all believers in Macedonia and Achaia [8]since it was from you that the word of the Lord started to spread - and not only throughout Macedonia and Achaia, for the news of your faith in God has spread everywhere. We do not need to tell other people about it: [9]other people tell us how we started the work among you, how you broke with idolatry when you were converted to God and became servants of the real, living God; [10]and how you are now waiting for Jesus, his Son, whom he raised from the dead, to come from heaven to save us from the retribution which is coming.

Paul's example in Thessalonika

2 [1]You know yourselves, my brothers, that our visit to you has not proved ineffectual.

[2]We had, as you know, been given rough treatment and been grossly insulted at Philippi, and it was our God who gave us the courage to proclaim his Good News to you in the face of great opposition. [3]We have not taken to preaching because we are deluded, or immoral, or trying to deceive anyone; [4]it was God who decided that we were fit to be entrusted with the Good News, and when we are speaking, we are not trying to please men but God, *who can read our inmost thoughts.*[a] [5]You know very well, and we can swear it before God, that never at any time have our speeches been simply flattery, or a cover for trying to get money; [6]nor have

---

[2a.] Jr 11:20.

we ever looked for any special honour from men, either from you or anybody else, [7]when we could have imposed ourselves on you with full weight, as apostles of Christ.

Instead, we were unassuming. Like a mother feeding and looking after her own children, [8]we felt so devoted and protective towards you, and had come to love you so much, that we were eager to hand over to you not only the Good News but our whole lives as well. [9]Let me remind you, brothers, how hard we used to work, slaving night and day so as not to be a burden on any one of you while we were proclaiming God's Good News to you. [10]You are witnesses, and so is God, that our treatment of you, since you became believers, has been impeccably right and fair. [11]You can remember how we treated every one of you as a father treats his children, [12]teaching you what was right, encouraging you and appealing to you to live a life worthy of God, who is calling you to share the glory of his kingdom.

The faith and the patience of the Thessalonians

[13]Another reason why we constantly thank God for you is that as soon as you heard the message that we brought you as God's message, you accepted it for what it really is, God's message and not some human thinking; and it is still a living power among you who believe it. [14]For you, my brothers, have been like the churches of God in Christ Jesus which are in Judaea, in suffering the same treatment from your own countrymen as they have

suffered from the Jews, [15]the people who put the Lord
Jesus to death, and the prophets too. And now they have
been persecuting us, and acting in a way that cannot
please God and makes them the enemies of the whole
human race, [16]because they are hindering us from
preaching to the pagans and trying to save them. They
never stop trying to *finish off the sins they have begun,*[b]
but retribution is overtaking them at last.

Paul's anxiety

[17]A short time after we had been separated from you - in
body but never in thought, brothers - we had an especially
strong desire and longing to see you face to face again,
[18]and we tried hard to come and visit you; I, Paul, tried
more than once, but Satan prevented us. [19]What do you
think is our pride and our joy? You are; and you will be *the
crown* of which we shall be *proudest* in the presence of our
Lord Jesus when he comes; [20]you are our pride and our joy.

Timothy's mission to Thessalonika

3 [1]When we could not bear the waiting any longer, we
decided it would be best to be left without a
companion at Athens, and [2]sent our brother Timothy, who
is God's helper in spreading the Good News of Christ, to
keep you firm and strong in the faith [3]and prevent any of

[2b] 2 M 6:14.

you from being unsettled by the present troubles. As you know, these are bound to come our way: [4]when we were with you, we warned you that we must expect to have persecutions to bear, and that is what has happened now, as you have found out. [5]That is why, when I could not stand waiting any longer, I sent to assure myself of your faith: I was afraid the Tempter[a] might have tried you too hard, and all our work might have been wasted.

Paul thanks God for good reports of the Thessalonians

[6]However, Timothy is now back from you and he has given us good news of your faith and your love, telling us that you always remember us with pleasure and want to see us quite as much as we want to see you. [7]And so, brothers, your faith has been a great comfort to us in the middle of our own troubles and sorrows; [8]now we can breathe again, as you are still holding firm in the Lord. [9]How can we thank God enough for you, for all the joy we feel before our God on your account? [10]We are earnestly praying night and day to be able to see you face to face again and make up any shortcomings in your faith.

[11]May God our Father himself, and our Lord Jesus Christ, make it easy for us to come to you. [12]May the Lord be generous in increasing your love and make you love one another and the whole human race as much as we love

---

[3a.] I.e. 'the one who puts you to the test'.

you. ¹³And may he so confirm your hearts in holiness that you may be blameless in the sight of our God and Father when our Lord Jesus Christ comes *with all his saints*.

Live in holiness and charity

4 ¹Finally, brothers, we urge you and appeal to you in the Lord Jesus to make more and more progress in the kind of life that you are meant to live: the life that God wants, as you learnt from us, and as you are already living it. ²You have not forgotten the instructions we gave you on the authority of the Lord Jesus.

³What God wants is for you all to be holy. He wants you to keep away from fornication, ⁴and each one of you to know how to use the body that belongs to him[a] in a way that is holy and honourable, ⁵not giving way to selfish lust like *the pagans who do not know God*.[b] ⁶He wants nobody at all ever to sin by taking advantage of a brother in these matters; the Lord always punishes sins of that sort, as we told you before and assured you. ⁷We have been called by God to be holy, not to be immoral; ⁸in other words, anyone who objects is not objecting to a human authority, but to God, *who gives you his* Holy *Spirit*.[c]

⁹As for loving our brothers, there is no need for anyone to write to you about that, since you have learnt from God

---

4a. Lit. 'the vessel that is his': either his own body or his wife's.
4b. Jr 10:25; Ps 79:6.   4c. Ezk 37:14.

yourselves to love one another, [10]and in fact this is what you are doing with all the brothers throughout the whole of Macedonia. However, we do urge you, brothers, to go on making even greater progress [11]and to make a point of living quietly, attending to your own business and earning your living, just as we told you to, [12]so that you are seen to be respectable by those outside the Church, though you do not have to depend on them.

The dead and the living at the time of the Lord's coming

[13]We want you to be quite certain, brothers, about those who have died,[d] to make sure that you do not grieve about them, like the other people who have no hope. [14]We believe that Jesus died and rose again, and that it will be the same for those who have died in Jesus: God will bring them with him. [15]We can tell you this from the Lord's own teaching, that any of us who are left alive until the Lord's coming will not have any advantage over those who have died. [16]At the trumpet of God, the voice of the archangel will call out the command and the Lord himself will come down from heaven; those who have died in Christ will be the first to rise, [17]and then those of us who are still alive will be taken up in the clouds, together with them, to meet the Lord in the air. So we shall stay with the Lord for ever. [18]With such thoughts as these you should comfort one another.

[4d.] Lit. 'those who are sleeping'.

Watchfulness while awaiting the coming of the Lord

5 ¹You will not be expecting us to write anything to you, brothers, about 'times and seasons', ²since you know very well that the Day of the Lord is going to come like a thief in the night. ³It is when people are saying, 'How quiet and peaceful it is' that the worst suddenly happens, as suddenly as labour pains come on a pregnant woman; and there will be no way for anybody to evade it.

⁴But it is not as if you live in the dark, my brothers, for that Day to overtake you like a thief. ⁵No, you are all sons of light and sons of the day: we do not belong to the night or to darkness, ⁶so we should not go on sleeping, as everyone else does, but stay wide awake and sober. ⁷Night is the time for sleepers to sleep and drunkards to be drunk, ⁸but we belong to the day and we should be sober; let us put on faith and love for a *breastplate*, and the hope of *salvation* for a *helmet*. ⁹God never meant us to experience the Retribution, but to win salvation through our Lord Jesus Christ, ¹⁰who died for us so that, alive or dead, we should still live united to him. ¹¹So give encouragement to each other, and keep strengthening one another, as you do already.

Some demands made by life in community

¹²We appeal to you, my brothers, to be considerate to those who are working amongst you and are above you in the Lord as your teachers. ¹³Have the greatest respect and affection for them because of their work.

Be at peace among yourselves. [14]And this is what we ask you to do, brothers: warn the idlers, give courage to those who are apprehensive, care for the weak and be patient with everyone. [15]Make sure that people do not try to take revenge; you must all think of what is best for each other and for the community. [16]Be happy at all times; [17]pray constantly; [18]and for all things give thanks to God, because this is what God expects you to do in Christ Jesus.

[19]Never try to suppress the Spirit [20]or treat the gift of prophecy with contempt; [21]think before you do anything - hold on to what is good [22]and *avoid every* form of *evil*.

Closing prayer and farewell

[23]May the God of peace make you perfect and holy; and may you all be kept safe and blameless, spirit, soul and body, for the coming of our Lord Jesus Christ. [24]God has called you and he will not fail you.

[25]Pray for us, my brothers.

[26]Greet all the brothers with the holy kiss. [27]My orders, in the Lord's name, are that this letter is to be read to all the brothers.

[28]The grace of our Lord Jesus Christ be with you.

❧ 2 THESSALONIANS ❧

THE SECOND LETTER OF PAUL TO THE CHURCH IN THESSALONIKA

Address

1 ¹From Paul, Silvanus and Timothy, to the Church in Thessalonika which is in God our Father and the Lord Jesus Christ; ²wishing you grace and peace from God the Father and the Lord Jesus Christ.

Thanksgiving and encouragement. The Last Judgement

³We feel we must be continually thanking God for you, brothers; quite rightly, because your faith is growing so wonderfully and the love that you have for one another never stops increasing; ⁴and among the churches of God we can take special pride in you for your constancy and faith under all the persecutions and troubles you have to bear. ⁵It all shows that God's judgement is just, and the purpose of it is that you may be found worthy of the kingdom of God; it is for the sake of this that you are suffering now.

⁶God will very rightly repay with injury those who are injuring you, ⁷and reward you, who are suffering now, with the same peace as he will give us, when the Lord

Jesus appears from heaven with the angels of his power. [8]He will come in *flaming fire* to impose the penalty on *all who do not acknowledge God*[a] and *refuse to accept* the Good News of our Lord Jesus. [9]It will be their punishment to be lost eternally, excluded *from the presence of the Lord and from the glory of his strength* [10]*on that day* when he comes *to be glorified among his saints* and *seen in his glory*[b] by all who believe in him; and you are believers, through our witness.

[11]Knowing this, we pray continually that our God will make you worthy of his call, and by his power fulfil all your desires for goodness and complete all that you have been doing through faith; [12]because in this way *the name* of our Lord Jesus Christ *will be glorified* in you and you in him, by the grace of our God and the Lord Jesus Christ.

The coming of the Lord and the prelude to it

2[1]To turn now, brothers, to the coming of our Lord Jesus Christ and how we shall all be gathered round him: [2]please do not get excited too soon or alarmed by any prediction or rumour or any letter claiming to come from us, implying that the Day of the Lord has already arrived. [3]Never let anyone deceive you in this way.

[1 a.] God's *coming in fire* is quoted from Is 66:15; the penalty on *those who do not acknowledge him* is a quotation from Jr 10:25.
[1 b.] Quotations from Is 2:10-17; 49:3; 66:5.

It cannot happen until the Great Revolt has taken place and the Rebel, the Lost One, has appeared. [4]This is the Enemy, the one who claims to be so much *greater than all* that men call 'god', so much greater than anything that is worshipped, that *he enthrones himself* in *God's* sanctuary and claims that he is God. [5]Surely you remember me telling you about this when I was with you? [6]And you know, too, what is still holding him back from appearing before his appointed time. [7]Rebellion is at its work already, but in secret, and the one who is holding it back has first to be removed [8]before the Rebel appears openly. The Lord *will kill him with the breath of his mouth*[a] and will annihilate him with his glorious appearance at his coming.

[9]But when the Rebel comes, Satan will set to work: there will be all kinds of miracles and a deceptive show of signs and portents, [10]and everything evil that can deceive those who are bound for destruction because they would not grasp the love of the truth which could have saved them. [11]The reason why God is sending a power to delude them and make them believe what is untrue [12]is to condemn all who refused to believe in the truth and chose wickedness instead.

Encouragement to persevere

[13]But we feel that we must be continually thanking God for you, brothers whom the Lord loves, because

---

[2a] Is 11:4.

God chose you from the beginning to be saved by the sanctifying Spirit and by faith in the truth. [14]Through the Good News that we brought he called you to this so that you should share the glory of our Lord Jesus Christ. [15]Stand firm, then, brothers, and keep the traditions that we taught you, whether by word of mouth or by letter. [16]May our Lord Jesus Christ himself, and God our Father who has given us his love and, through his grace, such inexhaustible comfort and such sure hope, [17]comfort you and strengthen you in everything good that you do or say.

3 [1]Finally, brothers, pray for us; pray that the Lord's message may spread quickly, and be received with honour as it was among you; [2]and pray that we may be preserved from the interference of bigoted and evil people, for faith is not given to everyone. [3]But the Lord is faithful, and he will give you strength and guard you from the evil one, [4]and we, in the Lord, have every confidence that you are doing and will go on doing all that we tell you. [5]May the Lord turn your hearts towards the love of God and the fortitude of Christ.

Against idleness and disunity

[6]In the name of the Lord Jesus Christ, we urge you, brothers, to keep away from any of the brothers who refuses to work or to live according to the tradition we passed on to you.

⁷You know how you are supposed to imitate us: now we were not idle when we were with you, ⁸nor did we ever have our meals at anyone's table without paying for them; no, we worked night and day, slaving and straining, so as not to be a burden on any of you. ⁹This was not because we had no right to be, but in order to make ourselves an example for you to follow.

¹⁰We gave you a rule when we were with you: not to let anyone have any food if he refused to do any work. ¹¹Now we hear that there are some of you who are living in idleness, doing no work themselves but interfering with everyone else's. ¹²In the Lord Jesus Christ, we order and call on people of this kind to go on quietly working and earning the food that they eat.

¹³My brothers, never grow tired of doing what is right. ¹⁴If anyone refuses to obey what I have written in this letter, take note of him and have nothing to do with him, so that he will feel that he is in the wrong; ¹⁵though you are not to regard him as an enemy but as a brother in need of correction.

Prayer and farewell wishes

¹⁶May the Lord of peace himself give you peace all the time and in every way. The Lord be with you all.

¹⁷From me, PAUL, these greetings in my own handwriting, which is the mark of genuineness in every letter; this is my own writing. ¹⁸May the grace of our Lord Jesus Christ be with you all.

❧ 1 Timothy ❧

The First Letter from Paul to Timothy

Address

1 ¹From Paul, apostle of Christ Jesus appointed by the command of God our saviour and of Christ Jesus our hope, ²to Timothy, true child of mine in the faith; wishing you grace, mercy and peace from God the Father and from Christ Jesus our Lord.

Suppress the false teachers

³As I asked you when I was leaving for Macedonia, please stay at Ephesus, to insist that certain people stop teaching strange doctrines ⁴and taking notice of myths and endless genealogies; these things are only likely to raise irrelevant doubts instead of furthering the designs of God which are revealed in faith. ⁵The only purpose of this instruction is that there should be love, coming out of a pure heart, a clear conscience and a sincere faith. ⁶There are some people who have gone off the straight course and taken a road that leads to empty speculation; ⁷they claim to be doctors of the Law but they understand neither the arguments they are using nor the opinions they are upholding.

The purpose of the Law

[8]We know, of course, that the Law is good, but only provided it is treated like any law, [9]in the understanding that laws are not framed for people who are good. On the contrary, they are for criminals and revolutionaries, for the irreligious and the wicked, for the sacrilegious and the irreverent; they are for people who kill their fathers or mothers and for murderers, [10]for those who are immoral with women or with boys or with men, for liars and for perjurers - and for everything else that is contrary to the sound teaching [11]that goes with the Good News of the glory of the blessed God, the gospel that was entrusted to me.

Paul on his own calling

[12]I thank Christ Jesus our Lord, who has given me strength, and who judged me faithful enough to call me into his service [13]even though I used to be a blasphemer and did all I could to injure and discredit the faith. Mercy, however, was shown me, because until I became a believer I had been acting in ignorance; [14]and the grace of our Lord filled me with faith and with the love that is in Christ Jesus. [15]Here is a saying that you can rely on and nobody should doubt: that Christ Jesus came into the world to save sinners. I myself am the greatest of them; [16]and if mercy has been shown to me, it is because Jesus Christ meant to make me the greatest evidence of

his inexhaustible patience for all the other people who would later have to trust in him to come to eternal life. [17]To the eternal King, the undying, invisible and only God, be honour and glory for ever and ever. Amen.

Timothy's responsibility

[18]Timothy, my son, these are the instructions that I am giving you: I ask you to remember the words once spoken over you by the prophets, and taking them to heart to fight like a good soldier [19]with faith and a good conscience for your weapons. Some people have put conscience aside and wrecked their faith in consequence. [20]I mean men like Hymenaeus and Alexander, whom I have handed over to Satan to teach them not to be blasphemous.

Liturgical prayer

2 [1]My advice is that, first of all, there should be prayers offered for everyone - petitions, intercessions and thanksgiving - [2]and especially for kings and others in authority, so that we may be able to live religious and reverent lives in peace and quiet. [3]To do this is right, and will please God our saviour: [4]he wants everyone to be saved and reach full knowledge of the truth. [5]For there is only one God, and there is only one mediator between God and mankind, himself a man, Christ Jesus, [6]who sacrificed himself as a ransom for them all. He is the evidence of this,

sent at the appointed time, and [7]I have been named a herald and apostle of it and - I am telling the truth and no lie - a teacher of the faith and the truth to the pagans.

[8]In every place, then, I want the men to lift their hands up reverently in prayer, with no anger or argument.

Women in the assembly

[9]Similarly, I direct that women are to wear suitable clothes and to be dressed quietly and modestly, without braided hair or gold and jewellery or expensive clothes; their adornment is [10]to do the sort of good works that are proper for women who profess to be religious. [11]During instruction, a woman should be quiet and respectful. [12]I am not giving permission for a woman to teach or to tell a man what to do. A woman ought not to speak, [13]because Adam was formed first and Eve afterwards, [14]and it was not Adam who was led astray but the woman who was led astray and fell into sin. [15]Nevertheless, she will be saved by childbearing, provided she lives a modest life and is constant in faith and love and holiness.

The elder-in-charge

3 [1]Here is a saying that you can rely on: To want to be a presiding elder[a] is to want to do a noble work. [2]That is

---

[3a]. The word *episcopos* used here by Paul had not yet acquired the same meaning as 'bishop'.

why the president must have an impeccable character. He must not have been married more than once, and he must be temperate, discreet and courteous, hospitable and a good teacher; ³not a heavy drinker, nor hot-tempered, but kind and peaceable. He must not be a lover of money. ⁴He must be a man who manages his own family well and brings his children up to obey him and be well-behaved: ⁵how can any man who does not understand how to manage his own family have responsibility for the church of God? ⁶He should not be a new convert, in case pride might turn his head and then he might be condemned as the devil was condemned. ⁷It is also necessary that people outside the Church should speak well of him, so that he never gets a bad reputation and falls into the devil's trap.

Deacons

⁸In the same way, deacons must be respectable men whose word can be trusted, moderate in the amount of wine they drink and with no squalid greed for money. ⁹They must be conscientious believers in the mystery of the faith. ¹⁰They are to be examined first, and only admitted to serve as deacons if there is nothing against them. ¹¹In the same way, the women must be respectable, not gossips but sober and quite reliable. ¹²Deacons must not have been married more than once, and must be men who manage their children and families well. ¹³Those of

them who carry out their duties well as deacons will earn a high standing for themselves and be rewarded with great assurance in their work for the faith in Christ Jesus.

The Church and the mystery of the spiritual life

[14]At the moment of writing to you, I am hoping that I may be with you soon; [15]but in case I should be delayed, I wanted you to know how people ought to behave in God's family - that is, in the Church of the living God, which upholds the truth and keeps it safe. [16]Without any doubt, the mystery of our religion is very deep indeed:

> He was made visible in the flesh,
> attested by the Spirit,
> seen by angels,
> proclaimed to the pagans,
> believed in by the world,
> taken up in glory.

False teachers

4 [1]The Spirit has explicitly said that during the last times there will be some who will desert the faith and choose to listen to deceitful spirits and doctrines that come from the devils; [2]and the cause of this is the lies told by hypocrites whose consciences are branded as though with a red-hot iron:[a] [3]they will say marriage is forbidden, and lay

---

[a] Like runaway slaves.

down rules about abstaining from foods which God created to be accepted with thanksgiving by all who believe and who know the truth.[b] ⁴Everything God has created is good, and no food is to be rejected, provided grace is said for it: ⁵the word of God and the prayer make it holy. ⁶If you put all this to the brothers, you will be a good servant of Christ Jesus and show that you have really digested the teaching of the faith and the good doctrine which you have always followed. ⁷Have nothing to do with godless myths and old wives' tales. Train yourself spiritually. ⁸'Physical exercises are useful enough, but the usefulness of spirituality is unlimited, since it holds out the reward of life here and now and of the future life as well'; ⁹that is a saying that you can rely on and nobody should doubt it. ¹⁰I mean that the point of all our toiling and battling is that we have put our trust in the living God and he is the saviour of the whole human race but particularly of all believers. ¹¹This is what you are to enforce in your teaching.

¹²Do not let people disregard you because you are young, but be an example to the believers in the way you speak and behave, and in your love, your faith and your purity. ¹³Make use of the time until I arrive by reading to the people, preaching and teaching. ¹⁴You have in you a spiritual gift which was given to you when the prophets

---

[b] The rejection of marriage was to be one of the hallmarks of Gnosticism; dietary regulations were more specifically Jewish.

spoke and the body of elders laid their hands on you; do not let it lie unused. [15]Think hard about all this, and put it into practice, and everyone will be able to see how you are advancing. [16]Take great care about what you do and what you teach; always do this, and in this way you will save both yourself and those who listen to you.

Pastoral practice

5 [1]Do not speak harshly to a man older than yourself, but advise him as you would your own father; treat the younger men as brothers [2]and older women as you would your mother. Always treat young women with propriety, as if they were sisters.

Widows

[3]Be considerate to widows; I mean those who are truly widows. [4]If a widow has children or grandchildren, they are to learn first of all to do their duty to their own families and repay their debt to their parents, because this is what pleases God. [5]But a woman who is really widowed and left without anybody can give herself up to God and consecrate all her days and nights to petitions and prayer. [6]The one who thinks only of pleasure is already dead while she is still alive: [7]remind them of all this, too, so that their lives may be blameless. [8]Anyone who does not look after his own relations, especially if they are living with him, has rejected the faith and is worse than an unbeliever.

⁹Enrolment as a widow is permissible only for a woman at least sixty years old who has had only one husband. ¹⁰She must be a woman known for her good works and for the way in which she has brought up her children, shown hospitality to strangers and washed the saints' feet, helped people who are in trouble and been active in all kinds of good work. ¹¹Do not accept young widows because if their natural desires get stronger than their dedication to Christ, they want to marry again, ¹²and then people condemn them for being unfaithful to their original promise. ¹³Besides, they learn how to be idle and go round from house to house; and then, not merely idle, they learn to be gossips and meddlers in other people's affairs, and to chatter when they would be better keeping quiet. ¹⁴I think it is best for young widows to marry again and have children and a home to look after, and not give the enemy any chance to raise a scandal about them; ¹⁵there are already some who have left us to follow Satan. ¹⁶If a Christian woman has widowed relatives, she should support them and not make the Church bear the expense but enable it to support those who are genuinely widows.

The elders

¹⁷The elders who do their work well while they are in charge are to be given double consideration, especially those who are assiduous in preaching and teaching. ¹⁸As

scripture says: *You must not muzzle an ox when it is treading out the corn;*[a] and again: *The worker deserves his pay*[b]. [19]Never accept any accusation brought against an elder unless it is supported *by two or three witnesses.* [20]If any of them are at fault, reprimand them publicly, as a warning to the rest. [21]Before God, and before Jesus Christ and the angels he has chosen, I put it to you as a duty to keep these rules impartially and never to be influenced by favouritism. [22]Do not be too quick to lay hands on any man, and never make yourself an accomplice in anybody else's sin; keep yourself pure.

[23]You should give up drinking only water and have a little wine for the sake of your digestion and the frequent bouts of illness that you have.

[24]The faults of some people are obvious long before anyone makes any complaint about them, while others have faults that are not discovered until afterwards. [25]In the same way, the good that people do can be obvious; but even when it is not, it cannot be hidden for ever.

Slaves

6 [1]All slaves 'under the yoke' must have unqualified respect for their masters, so that the name of God and our teaching are not brought into disrepute. [2]Slaves

---

[5a]. Dt 25:4. [5b]. Not traceable in the O.T.; but this is also to be found in Lk 10:7 where, again, it may be a quotation.

whose masters are believers are not to think any the less of them because they are brothers; on the contrary, they should serve them all the better, since those who have the benefit of their services are believers and dear to God.

The true teacher and the false teacher

This is what you are to teach them to believe and persuade them to do. ³Anyone who teaches anything different, and does not keep to the sound teaching which is that of our Lord Jesus Christ, the doctrine which is in accordance with true religion, ⁴is simply ignorant and must be full of self-conceit - with a craze for questioning everything and arguing about words. All that can come of this is jealousy, contention, abuse and wicked mistrust of one another; ⁵and unending disputes by people who are neither rational nor informed and imagine that religion is a way of making a profit. ⁶Religion, of course, does bring large profits, but only to those who are content with what they have. ⁷We brought nothing into the world, and we can take nothing out of it; ⁸but as long as we have food and clothing, let us be content with that. ⁹People who long to be rich are a prey to temptation; they get trapped into all sorts of foolish and dangerous ambitions which eventually plunge them into ruin and destruction. ¹⁰'The love of money is the root of all evils' and there are some who, pursuing it, have wandered away from the faith, and so given their souls any number of fatal wounds.

Timothy's vocation recalled

[11]But, as a man dedicated to God, you must avoid all that. You must aim to be saintly and religious, filled with faith and love, patient and gentle. [12]Fight the good fight of the faith and win for yourself the eternal life to which you were called when you made your profession and spoke up for the truth in front of many witnesses. [13]Now, before God the source of all life and before Christ, who spoke up as a witness for the truth in front of Pontius Pilate, I put to you the duty [14]of doing all that you have been told, with no faults or failures, until the Appearing of our Lord Jesus Christ,

[15]who at the due time will be revealed
by God, the blessed and only Ruler of all,
the King of kings and the Lord of lords,
[16]who alone is immortal,
whose home is in inaccessible light,
whom no man has seen and no man is able to see:
to him be honour and everlasting power. Amen.

Rich Christians

[17]Warn those who are rich in this world's goods that they are not to look down on other people; and not to set their hopes on money, which is untrustworthy, but on God who, out of his riches, gives us all that we need for our happiness. [18]Tell them that they are to do good, and be rich in good works, to be generous and willing to share - [19]this is the way they can save up a good capital sum for the future if they want to make sure of the only life that is real.

Final warning and conclusion

[20]My dear Timothy, take great care of all that has been entrusted to you. Have nothing to do with the pointless philosophical discussions and antagonistic beliefs of the 'knowledge' which is not knowledge at all; [21]by adopting this, some have gone right away from the faith. Grace be with you.

❧ 2 TIMOTHY ❧

THE SECOND LETTER FROM PAUL TO TIMOTHY

Greeting and thanksgiving

1 ¹From Paul, appointed by God to be an apostle of Christ Jesus in his design to promise life in Christ Jesus; ²to Timothy, dear child of mine, wishing you grace, mercy and peace from God the Father and from Christ Jesus our Lord.

³Night and day I thank God, keeping my conscience clear and remembering my duty to him as my ancestors did, and always I remember you in my prayers; I remember your tears ⁴and long to see you again to complete my happiness. ⁵Then I am reminded of the sincere faith which you have; it came first to live in your grandmother Lois, and your mother Eunice, and I have no doubt that it is the same faith in you as well.

The gifts that Timothy has received

⁶That is why I am reminding you now to fan into a flame the gift that God gave you when I laid my hands on you. ⁷God's gift was not a spirit of timidity, but the Spirit of power, and love, and self-control. ⁸So you are never to

be ashamed of witnessing to the Lord, or ashamed of me for being his prisoner; but with me, bear the hardships for the sake of the Good News, relying on the power of God [9]who has saved us and called us to be holy - not because of anything we ourselves have done but for his own purpose and by his own grace. This grace had already been granted to us, in Christ Jesus, before the beginning of time, [10]but it has only been revealed by the Appearing of our saviour Christ Jesus. He abolished death, and he has proclaimed life and immortality through the Good News; [11]and I have been named its herald, its apostle and its teacher.

[12]It is only on account of this that I am experiencing fresh hardships here now;[a] but I have not lost confidence, because I know who it is that I have put my trust in, and I have no doubt at all that he is able to take care of all that I have entrusted to him until that Day.

[13]Keep as your pattern the sound teaching you have heard from me, in the faith and love that are in Christ Jesus. [14]You have been trusted to look after something precious; guard it with the help of the Holy Spirit who lives in us.

[15]As you know, Phygelus and Hermogenes and all the others from Asia refuse to have anything more to do with me. [16]I hope the Lord will be kind to all the family of Onesiphorus, because he has often been a comfort to me and has never been ashamed of my chains. [17]On the contrary, as

---

[1 a.] The second imprisonment at Rome.

soon as he reached Rome, he really searched hard for me and found out where I was. [18]May it be the Lord's will that he shall find the Lord's mercy on that Day. You know better than anyone else how much he helped me at Ephesus.

How Timothy should face hardships

2 [1]Accept the strength, my dear son, that comes from the grace of Christ Jesus. [2]You have heard everything that I teach in public; hand it on to reliable people so that they in turn will be able to teach others.

[3]Put up with your share of difficulties, like a good soldier of Christ Jesus. [4]In the army, no soldier gets himself mixed up in civilian life, because he must be at the disposal of the man who enlisted him; [5]or take an athlete - he cannot win any crown unless he has kept all the rules of the contest; [6]and again, it is the working farmer who has the first claim on any crop that is harvested. [7]Think over what I have said, and the Lord will show you how to understand it all.

[8]Remember the Good News that I carry, 'Jesus Christ risen from the dead, sprung from the race of David'; [9]it is on account of this that I have my own hardships to bear, even to being chained like a criminal - but they cannot chain up God's news. [10]So I bear it all for the sake of those who are chosen, so that in the end they may have the salvation that is in Christ Jesus and the eternal glory that comes with it.

[11]Here is a saying that you rely on:

If we have died with him, then we shall live with him.
[12]If we hold firm, then we shall reign with him.
If we disown him, then he will disown us.
[13]We may be unfaithful, but he is always faithful,
for he cannot disown his own self.

The struggle against the immediate danger from false teachers

[14]Remind them of this; and tell them in the name of God that there is to be no wrangling about words: all that this ever achieves is the destruction of those who are listening. [15]Do all you can to present yourself in front of God as a man who has come through his trials, and a man who has no cause to be ashamed of his life's work and has kept a straight course with the message of the truth. [16]Have nothing to do with pointless philosophical discussions - they only lead further and further away from true religion. [17]Talk of this kind corrodes like gangrene, as in the case of Hymenaeus and Philetus, [18]the men who have gone right away from the truth and claim that the resurrection has already taken place. Some people's faith cannot stand up to them.

[19]However, God's solid foundation stone is still in position, and this is the inscription on it: *'The Lord knows those who are his own'*[a], and 'All who *call on the name of the Lord*[b] must avoid sin'.

[a.] Nb 16:5,26. [b.] Is 26:13.

²⁰Not all the dishes in a large house are made of gold and silver; some are made of wood or earthenware: some are kept for special occasions and others are for ordinary purposes. ²¹Now, to avoid these faults that I am speaking about is the Way for anyone to become a vessel for special occasions, fit for the Master himself to use, and kept ready for any good work.

²²Instead of giving in to your impulses like a young man, fasten your attention on holiness, faith, love and peace, in union with all those who call on the Lord with pure minds. ²³Avoid these futile and silly speculations, understanding that they only give rise to quarrels; ²⁴and a servant of the Lord is not to engage in quarrels, but has to be kind to everyone, a good teacher, and patient. ²⁵He has to be gentle when he corrects people who dispute what he says, never forgetting that God may give them a change of mind so that they recognise the truth and ²⁶come to their senses, once out of the trap where the devil caught them and kept them enslaved.

The dangers of the last days

3 ¹You may be quite sure that in the last days there are going to be some difficult times. ²People will be self-centred and grasping; boastful, arrogant and rude; disobedient to their parents, ungrateful, irreligious; ³heartless and unappeasable; they will be slanderers, profligates, savages and enemies of everything that is

good; [4]they will be treacherous and reckless and demented by pride, preferring their own pleasure to God. [5]They will keep up the outward appearance of religion but will have rejected the inner power of it. Have nothing to do with people like that.

[6]Of the same kind, too, are those men who insinuate themselves into families in order to get influence over silly women who are obsessed with their sins and follow one craze after another [7]in the attempt to educate themselves, but can never come to knowledge of the truth. [8]Men like this defy the truth just as Jannes and Jambres defied Moses:[a] their minds are corrupt and their faith spurious. [9]But they will not be able to go on any longer: their foolishness, like that of the other two, must become obvious to everybody.

[10]You know, though, what I have taught, how I have lived, what I have aimed at; you know my faith, my patience and my love; my constancy [11]and the persecutions and hardships that came to me in places like Antioch, Iconium and Lystra - all the persecutions I have endured; and the Lord has rescued me from every one of them. [12]You are well aware, then, that anybody who tries to live in devotion to Christ is certain to be attacked; [13]while these wicked impostors will go from bad to worse, deceiving others and deceived themselves.

[3 a.] In Jewish tradition, the leaders of the Egyptian magicians and disciples of Balaam.

[14]You must keep to what you have been taught and know to be true; remember who your teachers were, [15]and how, ever since you were a child, you have known the holy scriptures - from these you can learn the wisdom that leads to salvation through faith in Christ Jesus. [16]All scripture is inspired by God and can profitably be used for teaching, for refuting error, for guiding people's lives and teaching them to be holy. [17]This is how the man who is dedicated to God becomes fully equipped and ready for any good work.

A solemn charge

4 [1]Before God and before Christ Jesus who is to be judge of the living and the dead, I put this duty to you, in the name of his Appearing and of his kingdom: [2]proclaim the message and, welcome or unwelcome, insist on it. Refute falsehood, correct error, call to obedience - but do all with patience and with the intention of teaching. [3]The time is sure to come when, far from being content with sound teaching, people will be avid for the latest novelty and collect themselves a whole series of teachers according to their own tastes; [4]and then, instead of listening to the truth, they will turn to myths. [5]Be careful always to choose the right course; be brave under trials; make the preaching of the Good News your life's work, in thoroughgoing service.

Paul in the evening of his life

[6]As for me, my life is already being poured away as a libation, and the time has come for me to be gone. [7]I have fought the good fight to the end; I have run the race to the finish; I have kept the faith; [8]all there is to come now is the crown of righteousness reserved for me, which the Lord, the righteous judge, will give to me on that Day; and not only to me but to all those who have longed for his Appearing.

Final advice

[9]Do your best to come and see me as soon as you can. [10]As it is, Demas has deserted me for love of this life and gone to Thessalonika, Crescens has gone to Galatia and Titus to Dalmatia; [11]only Luke is with me. Get Mark to come and bring him with you; I find him a useful helper in my work. [12]I have sent Tychicus to Ephesus. [13]When you come, bring the cloak I left with Carpus in Troas, and the scrolls, especially the parchment ones. [14]Alexander the coppersmith has done me a lot of harm; *the Lord will repay him for what he has done*.[a] [15]Be on your guard against him yourself, because he has been bitterly contesting everything that we say.

[16]The first time I had to present my defence, there was not a single witness to support me. Every one of them deserted me - may they not be held accountable for it.

---

[a] Ps 28:4 and 62:12; Pr 24:12.

[17]But the Lord stood by me and gave me power, so that through me the whole message might be proclaimed for all the pagans to hear; and so I was *rescued from the lion's mouth*.[b] [18]The Lord will rescue me from all evil attempts on me, and bring me safely to his heavenly kingdom. To him be glory for ever and ever. Amen.

Farewells and final good wishes

[19]Greetings to Prisca and Aquila, and the family of Onesiphorus. [20]Erastus remained at Corinth, and I left Trophimus ill at Miletus. [21]Do your best to come before the winter.

Greetings to you from Eubulus, Pudens, Linus, Claudia and all the brothers. [22]The Lord be with your spirit. Grace be with you.

[4 b.] Ps 22:21.

❧ TITUS ❧

THE LETTER FROM PAUL TO TITUS

Address

1 ¹From Paul, servant of God, an apostle of Jesus Christ to bring those whom God has chosen to faith and to the knowledge of the truth that leads to true religion; ²and to give them the hope of the eternal life that was promised so long ago by God. He does not lie ³and so, at the appointed time, he revealed his decision, and, by the command of God our saviour, I have been commissioned to proclaim it. ⁴To Titus, true child of mine in the faith that we share, wishing you grace and peace from God the Father and from Christ Jesus our saviour.

The appointment of elders

⁵The reason I left you behind in Crete was for you to get everything organised there and appoint elders in every town, in the way that I told you: ⁶that is, each of them must be a man of irreproachable character; he must not have been married more than once, and his children must be believers and not uncontrollable or liable to be charged with disorderly conduct. ⁷Since, as president, he

will be God's representative, he must be irreproachable: never an arrogant or hot-tempered man, nor a heavy drinker or violent, nor out to make money; [8]but a man who is hospitable and a friend of all that is good; sensible, moral, devout and self-controlled; [9]and he must have a firm grasp of the unchanging message of the tradition, so that he can be counted on for both expounding the sound doctrine and refuting those who argue against it.

Opposing the false teachers

[10]And in fact you have there a great many people who need to be disciplined, who talk nonsense and try to make others believe it, particularly among those of the Circumcision. [11]They have got to be silenced: men of this kind ruin whole families, by teaching things that they ought not to, and doing it with the vile motive of making money. [12]It was one of themselves, one of their own prophets, who said,[a] 'Cretans were never anything but liars, dangerous animals and lazy': [13]and that is a true statement. So you will have to be severe in correcting them, and make them sound in the faith [14]so that they stop taking notice of Jewish myths and doing what they are told to do by people who are no longer interested in the truth.

[1 a.] Attributed to the Cretan poet Epimenides of Knossos.

¹⁵To all who are pure themselves, everything is pure; but to those who have been corrupted and lack faith, nothing can be pure - the corruption is both in their minds and in their consciences. ¹⁶They claim to have knowledge of God but the things they do are nothing but a denial of him; they are outrageously rebellious and quite incapable of doing good.

Some specific moral instruction

2 ¹It is for you, then, to preach the behaviour which goes with healthy doctrine. ²The older men should be reserved, dignified, moderate, sound in faith and love and constancy. ³Similarly, the older women should behave as though they were religious, with no scandalmongering and no habitual wine-drinking - they are to be the teachers of the right behaviour ⁴and show the younger women how they should love their husbands and love their children, ⁵how they are to be sensible and chaste, and how to work in their homes, and be gentle, and do as their husbands tell them, so that the message of God is never disgraced. ⁶In the same way, you have got to persuade the younger men to be moderate ⁷and in everything you do make yourself an example to them of working for good: when you are teaching, be an example to them in your sincerity and earnestness ⁸and in keeping all that you say so wholesome that nobody can make objections to it; and

213

then any opponent will be at a loss, with no accusation to make against us. [9]Tell the slaves that they are to be obedient to their masters and always do what they want without any argument; [10]and there must be no petty thieving - they must show complete honesty at all times, so that they are in every way a credit to the teaching of God our saviour.

The basis of the Christian moral life

[11]You see, God's grace has been revealed, and it has made salvation possible for the whole human race [12]and taught us that what we have to do is to give up everything that does not lead to God, and all our worldly ambitions; we must be self-restrained and live good and religious lives here in this present world, [13]while we are waiting in hope for the blessing which will come with the Appearing of the glory of our great God and saviour Christ Jesus.[a] [14]He sacrificed himself for us in order to *set us free from all wickedness*[b] and *to purify a people so that it could be his very own*[c] and would have no ambition except to do good.

[15]Now this is what you are to say, whether you are giving instruction or correcting errors; you can do so with full authority, and no one is to question it.

[2a.] Or 'our great God and our saviour, Christ Jesus'.   [2b.] Ps 130:8.
[2c.] Ex 19:5.

General instruction for believers

3 ¹Remind them that it is their duty to be obedient to the officials and representatives of the government; to be ready to do good at every opportunity; ²not to go slandering other people or picking quarrels, but to be courteous and always polite to all kinds of people. ³Remember, there was a time when we too were ignorant, disobedient and misled and enslaved by different passions and luxuries; we lived then in wickedness and ill-will, hating each other and hateful ourselves.

⁴But when the kindness and love of God our saviour for mankind were revealed, ⁵it was not because he was concerned with any righteous actions we might have done ourselves; it was for no reason except his own compassion that he saved us, by means of the cleansing water of rebirth and by renewing us with the Holy Spirit ⁶which he has so generously poured over us through Jesus Christ our saviour. ⁷He did this so that we should be justified by his grace, to become heirs looking forward to inheriting eternal life. ⁸This is doctrine that you can rely on.

Personal advice to Titus

I want you to be quite uncompromising in teaching all this, so that those who now believe in God may keep their minds constantly occupied in doing good works. All this is good, and will do nothing but good to everybody. ⁹But avoid pointless speculations, and those genealogies, and the quibbles and disputes about the Law - these are useless and can do no good to anyone. ¹⁰If a man disputes what you teach, then after a first and a second warning, have no more to do with him: ¹¹you will know that any man of that sort has already lapsed and condemned himself as a sinner.

Practical recommendations, farewells and good wishes

¹²As soon as I have sent Artemas or Tychicus to you, lose no time in joining me at Nicopolis, where I have decided to spend the winter. ¹³See to all the travelling arrangements for Zenas the lawyer and Apollos, and make sure they have everything they need. ¹⁴All our people are to learn to occupy themselves in doing good works for their practical needs as well, and not to be entirely unproductive.

¹⁵All those who are with me send their greetings. Greetings to those who love us in the faith. Grace be with you all.

❧ PHILEMON ❧

THE LETTER OF PAUL TO PHILEMON

Address

1 ¹From Paul, a prisoner of Christ Jesus and from our brother Timothy; to our dear fellow worker Philemon, ²our sister Apphia, our fellow soldier Archippus and the church that meets in your house; ³wishing you the grace and the peace of God our Father and the Lord Jesus Christ.

Thanksgiving and prayer

⁴I always mention you in my prayers and thank God for you, ⁵because I hear of the love and the faith which you have for the Lord Jesus and for all the saints. ⁶I pray that this faith will give rise to a sense of fellowship that will show you all the good things that we are able to do for Christ. ⁷I am so delighted, and comforted, to know of your love; they tell me, brother, how you have put new heart into the saints.

The request about Onesimus

⁸Now, although in Christ I can have no diffidence about telling you to do whatever is your duty, ⁹I am appealing to your love instead, reminding you that this is

Paul writing, an old man now and, what is more, still a prisoner of Christ Jesus. [10]I am appealing to you for a child of mine, whose father I became while wearing these chains: I mean Onesimus. [11]He was of no use to you before, but he will be useful[a] to you now, as he has been to me. [12]I am sending him back to you, and with him - I could say - a part of my own self. [13]I should have liked to keep him with me; he could have been a substitute for you, to help me while I am in the chains that the Good News has brought me. [14]However, I did not want to do anything without your consent; it would have been forcing your act of kindness, which should be spontaneous. [15]I know you have been deprived of Onesimus for a time, but it was only so that you could have him back for ever, [16]not as a slave any more, but something much better than a slave, a dear brother; especially dear to me, but how much more to you, as a blood-brother as well as a brother in the Lord. [17]So if all that we have in common means anything to you, welcome him as you would me; [18]but if he has wronged you in any way or owes you anything, then let me pay for it. [19]I am writing this in my own handwriting: I, Paul, shall pay it back - I will not add any mention of your own debt to me, which is yourself. [20]Well then, brother, I am counting on

---

[1a.] A pun - 'Onesimus' means 'useful'.

you, in the Lord; put new heart into me, in Christ. ²¹I am writing with complete confidence in your compliance, sure that you will do even more than I ask.

A personal request. Good wishes

²²There is another thing: will you get a place ready for me to stay in? I am hoping through your prayers to be restored to you.

²³Epaphras, a prisoner with me in Christ Jesus, sends his greetings; ²⁴so do my colleagues Mark, Aristarchus, Demas and Luke.

²⁵May the grace of our Lord Jesus Christ be with your spirit.

THE LETTER TO THE
❧ HEBREWS ❧

A LETTER ADDRESSED TO A
JEWISH-CHRISTIAN COMMUNITY

PROLOGUE

The greatness of the incarnate Son of God

1 ¹At various times in the past and in various different ways, God spoke to our ancestors through the prophets; but ²in our own time, the last days, he has spoken to us through his Son, the Son that he has appointed to inherit everything and through whom he made everything there is. ³He is the radiant light of God's glory and the perfect copy of his nature, sustaining the universe by his powerful command; and now that he has destroyed the defilement of sin, he has gone to take his place in heaven at the right hand of divine Majesty. ⁴So he is now as far above the angels as the title which he has inherited is higher than their own name.

I. THE SON IS GREATER THAN THE ANGELS

Proof from the scriptures

[5]God has never said to any angel: *You are my Son, today I have become your father;*[a] or: *I will be a father to him and he a son to me.*[b] [6]Again, when he brings the First-born into the world, he says: *Let all the angels of God worship him.*[c] [7]About the angels, he says: *He makes his angels winds and his servants flames of fire,*[d] [8]but to his Son he says: *God, your throne shall last for ever and ever;* and: *his royal sceptre is the sceptre of virtue;* [9]*virtue you love as much as you hate wickedness. This is why God, your God, has anointed you with the oil of gladness, above all your rivals.*[e] [10]And again: *It is you, Lord, who laid earth's foundations in the beginning, the heavens are the work of your hands;* [11]*all will vanish, though you remain, all wear out like a garment;* [12]*you will roll them up like a cloak, and* like a garment *they will be changed. But yourself, you never change and your years are unending.*[f] [13]God has never said to any angel: *Sit at my right hand and I will make your enemies a footstool for you.*[g] [14]The truth is they are all spirits whose work is service, sent to help those who will be the heirs of salvation.

[a.] Ps 2:7.   [b.] 2 S 7:14.   [c.] Dt 32:43.   [d.] Ps 104:4.   [e.] Ps 45:6-7.
[f.] Ps 102:25-27.   [g.] Ps 110:1.

An exhortation

2 [1]We ought, then, to turn our minds more attentively than before to what we have been taught, so that we do not drift away. [2]If a promise that was made through angels[a] proved to be so true that every infringement and disobedience brought its own proper punishment, [3]then we shall certainly not go unpunished if we neglect this salvation that is promised to us. The promise was first announced by the Lord himself, and is guaranteed to us by those who heard him; [4]God himself confirmed their witness with signs and marvels and miracles of all kinds, and by freely giving the gifts of the Holy Spirit.

Redemption brought by Christ, not by angels

[5]He did not appoint angels to be rulers of the world to come, and that world is what we are talking about. [6]Somewhere there is a passage that shows us this. It runs: *What is man that you should spare a thought for him, the son of man that you should care for him?* [7]*For a short while you made him lower than the angels; you crowned him with glory and splendour.* [8]*You have put him in command of everything.*[b] Well then, if he has *put him in command of everything*, he has left nothing which is not under his command. At present, it is true, we are not able to see that *everything has been put under his command,*

[2a] The Law.   [2b] Ps 8:4-6 (LXX).

[9]but we do see in Jesus one who was *for a short while made lower than the angels* and is now *crowned with glory and splendour* because he submitted to death; by God's grace he had to experience death for all mankind.

[10]As it was his purpose to bring a great many of his sons into glory, it was appropriate that God, for whom everything exists and through whom everything exists, should make perfect, through suffering, the leader who would take them to their salvation. [11]For the one who sanctifies, and the ones who are sanctified, are of the same stock; that is why he openly calls them *brothers* [12]in the text: *I shall announce your name to my brothers, praise you in full assembly;*[c] or the text: [13]*In him I hope;* or the text: *Here I am with the children whom God has given me.*[d]

[14]Since all the *children* share the same blood and flesh, he too shared equally in it, so that by his death he could take away all the power of the devil, who had power over death, [15]and set free all those who had been held in slavery all their lives by the fear of death. [16]For it was not the angels that he took to himself; he took to himself *descent from Abraham.*[e] [17]It was essential that he should in this way become completely like his brothers so that he could be a compassionate and trustworthy high priest of

---

[2 c.] Ps 22:22.   [2 d.] This, and the previous text, are from Is 8:17-18.
[2 e.] Is 41:8-9.

God's religion, able to atone for human sins. [18]That is, because he has himself been through temptation he is able to help others who are tempted.

II. JESUS THE FAITHFUL AND MERCIFUL HIGH PRIEST

Christ higher than Moses

3 [1]That is why all you who are holy brothers and have had the same heavenly call should turn your minds to Jesus, the apostle and the high priest of our religion. [2]He was *faithful* to the one who appointed him, just like *Moses,* who stayed faithful *in all his house;* [3]but he has been found to deserve a greater glory than Moses. It is the difference between the honour given to the man that built the house and to the house itself. [4]Every house is built by someone, of course; but God built everything that exists. [5]It is true that Moses was *faithful in the house* of God, as a servant, acting as witness to the things which were to be divulged later; [6]but Christ was faithful as a son, and as the master in the house. And we are his house, as long as we cling to our hope with the confidence that we glory in.

How to reach God's land of rest

[7]The Holy Spirit says: *If only you would listen to him today;* [8]*do not harden your hearts, as happened in the Rebellion, on the Day of Temptation in the*

wilderness, [9]*when your ancestors challenged me and tested me, though they had seen what I could do* [10]*for forty years. That was why I was angry with that generation and said: How unreliable these people who refuse to grasp my ways!* [11]*And so, in anger, I swore that not one would reach the place of rest I had for them.*[a] [12]Take care, brothers, that there is not in any one of your community a wicked mind, so unbelieving as to turn away from the living God. [13]Every day, as long as this 'today' lasts, keep encouraging one another so that none of you is *hardened* by the lure of sin, [14]because we shall remain co-heirs with Christ only if we keep a grasp on our first confidence right to the end. [15]In this saying: *If only you would listen to him today; do not harden your hearts, as happened in the Rebellion,* [16]those who *rebelled* after they had *listened* were all the people who were brought out of Egypt by Moses. [17]And those who made God *angry for forty years* were the ones who sinned and whose *dead bodies were left lying in the wilderness.*[b] [18]Those that he *swore would never reach the place of rest he had for them* were those who had been disobedient. [19]We see, then, that it was because they were unfaithful that they were not able to reach it.

[3a.] Ps 95. [3b.] Nb 14:29.

4 ¹Be careful, then: the promise of *reaching the place of rest he had for them* still holds good, and none of you must think that he has come too late for it. ²We received the Good News exactly as they did; but hearing the message did them no good because they did not share the faith of those who listened. ³We, however, who have faith, shall reach a place of rest, as in the text: *And so, in anger, I swore that not one would reach the place of rest I had for them.* God's work was undoubtedly all finished at the beginning of the world; ⁴as one text says, referring to the seventh day: *After all his work God rested on the seventh day.*ᵃ ⁵The text we are considering says: *They shall not reach the place of rest I had for them.* ⁶It is established, then, that there would be some people who would reach it, and since those who first heard the Good News failed to reach it through their disobedience, ⁷God fixed another day when, much later, he said 'today' through David in the text already quoted: *If only you would listen to him today; do not harden your hearts.* ⁸If Joshua had led them into this place of rest, God would not later on have spoken so much of another day. ⁹There must still be, therefore, a place of rest reserved for God's people, the seventh-day rest, ¹⁰since to *reach the place of rest* is to *rest after your work,* as God did after his. ¹¹We

---

⁴ᵃ· Gn 2:2.

must therefore do everything we can to *reach this place of rest,* or some of you might copy this example of disobedience and be lost.

The word of God and Christ the priest

¹²The word of God is something alive and active: it cuts like any double-edged sword but more finely: it can slip through the place where the soul is divided from the spirit, or joints from the marrow; it can judge the secret emotions and thoughts. ¹³No created thing can hide from him; everything is uncovered and open to the eyes of the one to whom we must give account of ourselves.

¹⁴Since in Jesus, the Son of God, we have the supreme high priest who has gone through to the highest heaven, we must never let go of the faith that we have professed. ¹⁵For it is not as if we had a high priest who was incapable of feeling our weaknesses with us; but we have one who has been tempted in every way that we are, though he is without sin. ¹⁶Let us be confident, then, in approaching the throne of grace, that we shall have mercy from him and find grace when we are in need of help.

Jesus the compassionate high priest

5 ¹Every high priest has been taken out of mankind and is appointed to act for men in their relations with God, to offer gifts and sacrifices for sins; and so ²he can sympathise with those who are ignorant or uncertain

because he too lives in the limitations of weakness. ³That is why he has to make sin offerings for himself as well as for the people. ⁴No one takes this honour on himself, but each one is called by God, as Aaron was. ⁵Nor did Christ give himself the glory of becoming high priest, but he had it from the one who said to him: *You are my son, today I have become your father,*[a] ⁶and in another text: *You are a priest of the order of Melchizedek, and for ever.*[b] ⁷During his life on earth, he offered up prayer and entreaty, aloud and in silent tears, to the one who had the power to save him out of death, and he submitted so humbly that his prayer was heard. ⁸Although he was Son, he learnt to obey through suffering; ⁹but having been made perfect, he became for all who obey him the source of eternal salvation ¹⁰and was acclaimed by God with the title of high priest *of the order of Melchizedek.*

III. THE AUTHENTIC PRIESTHOOD
OF JESUS CHRIST

Christian life and theology

¹¹On this subject we have many things to say, and they are difficult to explain because you have grown so slow at understanding. ¹²Really, when you should by this time have become masters, you need someone to teach

---

[a] Ps 2:7.   [b] Ps 110:4.

you all over again the elementary principles of interpreting God's oracles; you have gone back to needing milk, and not solid food. ¹³Truly, anyone who is still living on milk cannot digest the doctrine of righteousness because he is still a baby. ¹⁴Solid food is for mature men with minds trained by practice to distinguish between good and bad.

The author explains his intention

6 ¹Let us leave behind us then all the elementary teaching about Christ and concentrate on its completion, without going over the fundamental doctrines again: the turning away from dead actions and towards faith in God; ²the teaching about baptisms and the laying-on of hands; the teaching about the resurrection of the dead and eternal judgement. ³This, God willing, is what we propose to do.

⁴As for those people who were once brought into the light, and tasted the gift from heaven, and received a share of the Holy Spirit, ⁵and appreciated the good message of God and the powers of the world to come ⁶and yet in spite of this have fallen away - it is impossible for them to be renewed a second time. They cannot be repentant if they have wilfully crucified the Son of God and openly mocked him. ⁷A field that has been well watered by frequent rain, and gives the crops that are wanted by the owners who grew them, is given

God's blessing; [8]but one that grows brambles and thistles is abandoned, and practically cursed. It will end by being burnt.

Words of hope and encouragement

[9]But you, my dear people - in spite of what we have just said, we are sure you are in a better state and on the way to salvation. [10]God would not be so unjust as to forget all you have done, the love that you have for his name or the services you have done, and are still doing, for the saints.[a] [11]Our one desire is that every one of you should go on showing the same earnestness to the end, to the perfect fulfilment of our hopes, [12]never growing careless, but imitating those who have the faith and the perseverance to inherit the promises.

[13]When God made the promise to Abraham, he *swore by his own self,* since it was impossible for him to swear by anyone greater: [14]*I will shower blessings on you and give you many descendants.*[b] [15]Because of that, Abraham persevered and saw the promise fulfilled. [16]Men, of course, swear an oath by something greater than themselves, and between men, confirmation by an oath puts an end to all dispute. [17]In the same way, when God wanted to make the heirs to the promise thoroughly realise that his purpose was unalterable, he conveyed this by an oath; [18]so that

---

[a] The same phrase is used in Rm and 2 Co about a collection of money made for the church in Jerusalem. [b] Gn 22.

there would be two unalterable things in which it was impossible for God to be lying, and so that we, now we have found safety, should have a strong encouragement to take a firm grip on the hope that is held out to us. [19]Here we have an anchor for our soul, as sure as it is firm, and reaching right *through beyond the veil*[c] [20]where Jesus has entered before us and on our behalf, to become a high *priest of the order of Melchizedek, and for ever.*

A. CHRIST'S PRIESTHOOD HIGHER THAN LEVITICAL PRIESTHOOD

Melchizedek[a]

7 [1]You remember that *Melchizedek, king of Salem, a priest of God Most High, went to meet Abraham who was on his way back after defeating the kings,* and *blessed him;* [2]and also that it was to him that Abraham gave *a tenth of all that he had.* By the interpretation of his name, he is, first, 'king of righteousness' and also *king of Salem,* that is, 'king of peace'; [3]he has no father, mother or ancestry, and his life has no beginning or ending; he is like the Son of God. He remains a priest for ever.

---

[6] c. Lv 16:2.
[7] a. Gn 14, from which the following quotation is made, is silent about any ancestors or descendants of Melchizedek, and about 'the beginning and ending' of his life.

Melchizedek accepted tithes from Abraham

⁴Now think how great this man must have been, if the patriarch *Abraham paid him a tenth of the treasure he had captured.*ᵇ ⁵We know that any of the descendants of Levi who are admitted to the priesthood are obliged by the Law to take tithes from the people, and this is taking them from their own brothers although they too are descended from Abraham. ⁶But this man, who was not of the same descent, took his tenth from Abraham, and he gave his blessing to the holder of the promises. ⁷Now it is indisputable that a blessing is given by a superior to an inferior. ⁸Further, in the one case it is ordinary mortal men who receive the tithes, and in the other, someone who is declared to be still alive. ⁹It could be said that Levi himself, who receives tithes, actually paid them, in the person of Abraham, ¹⁰because he was still in the loins of his ancestor when *Melchizedek came to meet him.*

From levitical priesthood to the priesthood of Melchizedek

¹¹Now if perfection had been reached through the levitical priesthood because the Law given to the nation rests on it, why was it still necessary for a new priesthood to arise, one *of the same order as Melchizedek*ᶜ not

---

⁷ᵇ. The regular tithe paid to levitical priests was a tenth. ⁷ᶜ. Ps 110:4.

counted as being 'of the same order as' Aaron? [12]But any change in the priesthood must mean a change in the Law as well.

[13]So our Lord, of whom these things were said, belonged to a different tribe, the members of which have never done service at the altar; [14]everyone knows he came from Judah, a tribe which Moses did not even mention when dealing with priests.

The abrogation of the old Law

[15]This[d] becomes even more clearly evident when there appears a second Melchizedek, who is a priest [16]not by virtue of a law about physical descent, but by the power of an indestructible life. [17]For it was about him that the prophecy was made: *You are a priest of the order of Melchizedek, and for ever.* [18]The earlier commandment is thus abolished, because it was neither effective nor useful, [19]since the Law could not make anyone perfect; but now this commandment is replaced by something better - the hope that brings us nearer to God.

Christ's priesthood is unchanging

[20]What is more, this was not done without the taking of an oath. The others, indeed, were made priests without any oath; [21]but he with an oath sworn by the one who

---

[7 d.] What has been said in v.12.

declared to him: *The Lord has sworn an oath which he will never retract: you are a priest, and for ever.*[e] [22]And it follows that it is a greater covenant for which Jesus has become our guarantee. [23]Then there used to be a great number of those other priests, because death put an end to each one of them; [24]but this one, because he remains *for ever,* can never lose his priesthood. [25]It follows, then, that his power to save is utterly certain, since he is living for ever to intercede for all who come to God through him.

The perfection of the heavenly high priest

[26]To suit us, the ideal high priest would have to be holy, innocent and uncontaminated, beyond the influence of sinners, and raised up above the heavens; [27]one who would not need to offer sacrifices every day, as the other high priests do for their own sins and then for those of the people, because he has done this once and for all by offering himself. [28]The Law appoints high priests who are men subject to weakness; but the promise on oath, which came after the Law, appointed the Son who is made perfect *for ever.*

[7e] Ps 110:4.

B. THE SUPERIORITY OF THE WORSHIP, THE SANCTUARY AND THE MEDIATION PROVIDED BY CHRIST THE PRIEST

The new priesthood and the new sanctuary

8 [1]The great point of all that we have said is that we have a high priest of exactly this kind. He has his place *at the right* of the throne of divine Majesty in the heavens, [2]and he is the minister of the sanctuary and of the true *Tent* of Meeting which *the Lord,* and not any man, *set up.*[a] [3]It is the duty of every high priest to offer gifts and sacrifices, and so this one too must have something to offer. [4]In fact, if he were on earth, he would not be a priest at all, since there are others who make the offerings laid down by the Law [5]and these only maintain the service of a model or a reflection of the heavenly realities. For Moses, when he had the Tent to build, was warned by God who said: *See that you make everything according to the pattern shown you on the mountain.*[b]

Christ is the mediator of a greater covenant

[6]We have seen that he has been given a ministry of a far higher order, and to the same degree it is a better covenant of which he is the mediator, founded on better promises. [7]If that first covenant had been without a fault, there would have been no need for a second one to replace it. [8]And in fact God does find fault with them; he says:

[8a]. Nb 24:6 (LXX) . [8b]. Ex 25:40.

See, the days are coming - it is the Lord who speaks -
when I will establish a new covenant
with the House of Israel and the House of Judah,
⁹but not a covenant like the one I made with their
    ancestors
on the day I took them by the hand
to bring them out of the land of Egypt.
They abandoned that covenant of mine,
and so I on my side deserted them. It is the Lord
    who speaks.
¹⁰No, this is the covenant I will make
with the House of Israel
when those days arrive - it is the Lord who speaks.
I will put my laws into their minds
and write them on their hearts.
Then I will be their God
and they shall be my people.
¹¹There will be no further need for neighbour to try
    to teach neighbour,
or brother to say to brother,
'Learn to know the Lord'.
No, they will all know me,
the least no less than the greatest,
¹²since I will forgive their iniquities
*and never call their sins to mind.*ᶜ

---

8 c. Jr 31:31-34.

¹³By speaking of a *new* covenant, he implies that the first one is already old. Now anything old only gets more antiquated until in the end it disappears.

Christ enters the heavenly sanctuary

9 ¹The first covenant also had its laws governing worship, and its sanctuary, a sanctuary on this earth. ²There was a tent which comprised two compartments: the first, in which the lamp-stand, the table and the presentation loaves were kept, was called the Holy Place; ³then beyond the second veil, an innermost part which was called the Holy of Holies ⁴to which belonged the gold altar of incense, and the ark of the covenant, plated all over with gold. In this were kept the gold jar containing the manna, Aaron's branch that grew the buds, and the stone tablets of the covenant. ⁵On top of it was the throne of mercy, and outspread over it were the glorious cherubs. This is not the time to go into greater detail about this.

⁶Under these provisions, priests are constantly going into the outer tent to carry out their acts of worship, ⁷but the second tent is entered only once a year, and then only by the high priest who must go in by himself and take the blood to offer for his own faults and the people's. ⁸By this, the Holy Spirit is showing that no one has the right to go into the sanctuary as long as the outer tent remains standing; ⁹it is a symbol for this present time. None of the gifts and sacrifices offered under these regulations can

possibly bring any worshipper to perfection in his inner self; [10]they are rules about the outward life, connected with foods and drinks and washing at various times, intended to be in force only until it should be time to reform them.

[11]But now Christ has come, as the high priest of all the blessings which were to come. He has passed through the greater, the more perfect tent, which is better than the one made by men's hands because it is not of this created order; [12]and he has entered the sanctuary once and for all, taking with him not the blood of goats and bull calves, but his own blood, having won an eternal redemption for us. [13]The blood of goats and bulls and the ashes of a heifer are sprinkled on those who have incurred defilement and they restore the holiness of their outward lives; [14]how much more effectively the blood of Christ, who offered himself as the perfect sacrifice to God through the eternal Spirit, can purify our inner self from dead actions so that we do our service to the living God.

Christ seals the new covenant with his blood

[15]He brings a new covenant, as the mediator, only so that the people who were called to an eternal inheritance may actually receive what was promised: his death took place to cancel the sins that infringed the earlier covenant. [16]Now wherever a will is in question, the death of the testator must be established; [17]indeed, it only becomes

valid with that death, since it is not meant to have any effect while the testator is still alive. [18]That explains why even the earlier covenant needed is something to be killed in order to take effect, [19]and why, after Moses had announced all the commandments of the Law to the people, he took the calves' blood, the goats' blood and some water, and with these he sprinkled the book itself and all the people, using scarlet wool and hyssop; [20]saying as he did so: *This is the blood of the covenant that God has laid down for you.*[a] [21]After that, he sprinkled the tent and all the liturgical vessels with blood in the same way. [22]In fact, according to the Law almost everything has to be purified[b] with blood; and if there is no shedding of blood, there is no remission. [23]Obviously, only the copies of heavenly things can be purified in this way, and the heavenly things themselves have to be purified by a higher sort of sacrifice than this. [24]It is not as though Christ had entered a man-made sanctuary which was only modelled on the real one; but it was heaven itself, so that he could appear in the actual presence of God on our behalf. [25]And he does not have to offer himself again and again, like the high priest going into the sanctuary year after year with the blood that is not his own, [26]or else he would have had to suffer over and over again since the world began. Instead of that, he has made his appearance once and for

---

[9a.] Ex 24:8.   [9b.] Many instances are given in Lv.

all, now at the end of the last age, to do away with sin by sacrificing himself. [27]Since men only die once, and after that comes judgement, [28]so Christ, too, offers himself only once *to take the faults of many on himself*,[c] and when he appears a second time, it will not be to deal with sin but to reward with salvation those who are waiting for him.

SUMMARY: CHRIST'S SACRIFICE SUPERIOR TO THE SACRIFICES OF THE MOSAIC LAW

The old sacrifices ineffective

10 [1]So, since the Law has no more than a *reflection* of these realities, and no finished picture of them, it is quite incapable of bringing the worshippers to perfection, with the same sacrifices repeatedly offered year after year. [2]Otherwise, the offering of them would have stopped, because the worshippers, when they had been purified once, would have no awareness of sins. [3]Instead of that, the sins are recalled year after year in the sacrifices. [4]Bulls' blood and goats' blood are useless for taking away sins, [5]and this is what he said, on coming into the world:

> *You who wanted no sacrifice or oblation,*
> *prepared a body for me.*
> [6]*You took no pleasure in holocausts or sacrifices for sin;*
> [7]*then I said,*

---

[9][c.] Is 53:12.

just as I was commanded in the scroll of the book,
'God, here I am! I am coming to obey your will.'[a]

[8]Notice that he says first: *You did not want* what the Law lays down as the things to be offered, that is: *the sacrifices, the oblations, the holocausts and the sacrifices for sin,* and *you took no pleasure* in them; [9]and then he says: *Here I am! I am coming to obey your will.* He is abolishing the first sort to replace it with the second. [10]And this *will* was for us to be made holy by the *offering* of his *body* made once and for all by Jesus Christ.

The efficacy of Christ's sacrifice

[11]All the priests stand at their duties every day, offering over and over again the same sacrifices which are quite incapable of taking sins away. [12]He, on the other hand, has offered one single sacrifice for sins, and then taken his place forever, *at the right hand of God,* [13]where he is now waiting *until his enemies are made into a footstool for him.*[b] [14]By virtue of that one single offering, he has achieved the eternal perfection of all whom he is sanctifying. [15]The Holy Spirit assures us of this; for he says, first:

[16]*This is the covenant I will make with them*
when those days arrive;[c]

and the Lord then goes on to say:

---

10 a. Ps 40:6-8 (LXX).   10 b. Ps 110.   10 c. From the long quotation from Jr 31 made in ch. 8.

> *I will put my laws into their hearts*
> *and write them on their minds.*
> [17]*I will never call their sins to mind,*
> *or their offences.*

[18]When all sins have been forgiven, there can be no more sin offerings.

IV. PERSEVERING FAITH

The Christian opportunity

[19]In other words, brothers, through the blood of Jesus we have the right to enter the sanctuary, [20]by a new way which he has opened for us, a living opening through the curtain, that is to say, his body. [21]And we have the *supreme high priest* over all *the house of God*. [22]So as we go in, let us be sincere in heart and filled with faith, our minds sprinkled and free from any trace of bad conscience and our bodies washed with pure water. [23]Let us keep firm in the hope we profess, because the one who made the promise is faithful. [24]Let us be concerned for each other, to stir a response in love and good works. [25]Do not stay away from the meetings of the community, as some do, but encourage each other to go; the more so as you see the Day drawing near.

The danger of apostasy

[26]If, after we have been given knowledge of the truth, we should deliberately commit any sins, then there is no

longer any sacrifice for them. [27]There will be left only the dreadful prospect of judgement and of *the raging fire* that is to *burn rebels.*[d] [28]Anyone who disregards the Law of Moses is ruthlessly *put to death on the word of two witnesses or three;*[e] [29]and you may be sure that anyone who tramples on the Son of God, and who treats *the blood of the covenant* which sanctified him as if it were not holy, and who insults the Spirit of grace, will be condemned to a far severer punishment. [30]We are all aware who it was that said: *Vengeance is mine; I will repay.*[f] And again: *The Lord will judge his people.* [31]It is a dreadful thing to fall into the hands of the living God.

Motives for perseverance

[32]Remember all the sufferings that you had to meet after you received the light, in earlier days; [33]sometimes by being yourselves publicly exposed to insults and violence, and sometimes as associates of others who were treated in the same way. [34]For you not only shared in the sufferings of those who were in prison, but you happily accepted being stripped of your belongings, knowing that you owned something that was better and lasting. [35]Be as confident now, then, since the reward is so great. [36]You will need endurance to do God's will and gain what he has promised.

[10d.] Is 26:11 (LXX).   [10e.] Dt 17:6.   [10f.] Dt 32:35-36.

> [37]Only a little while now, a very little while,
>   and the one that is coming will have come; he will
>   not delay.[g]
> [38]The righteous man will live by faith,
>   but if he draws back, my soul will take no pleasure
>   in him.[h]

[39]You and I are not the sort of people who *draw back*, and are lost by it; we are the sort who keep *faithful* until our souls are saved.

The exemplary faith of our ancestors

11 [1]Only faith can guarantee the blessings that we hope for, or prove the existence of the realities that at present remain unseen. [2]It was for faith that our ancestors were commended.

[3]It is by faith that we understand that the world was created by one word from God, so that no apparent cause can account for the things we can see.

[4]It was because of his faith that Abel offered God a better sacrifice than Cain, and for that he was declared to be righteous when *God* made acknowledgement of *his offerings*. Though he is dead, he still speaks by faith.

[5]It was because of his faith that Enoch was taken up and did not have to experience death: *he was not to be found because God had taken him*.[a] This was because

---

[10 g] Is 26:20 (LXX).   [10 h] Hab 2:3-4 (LXX).
[11 a] Gn 5:24.

before his assumption it is attested that *he had pleased God.* 6Now it is impossible to please God without faith, since anyone who comes to him must believe that he exists and rewards those who try to find him.

7It was through his faith that Noah, when he had been warned by God of something that had never been seen before, felt a holy fear and built an ark to save his family. By his faith the world was convicted, and he was able to claim the righteousness which is the reward of faith.

8It was by faith that Abraham obeyed the call to *set out* for a country that was the inheritance given to him and his descendants, and that *he set out* without knowing where he was going. 9By faith he arrived, *as a foreigner*, in the Promised Land, and lived there as if in a strange country, with Isaac and Jacob, who were heirs with him of the same promise. 10They lived there in tents while he looked forward to a city founded, designed and built by God.

11It was equally by faith that Sarah, in spite of being past the age, was made able to conceive, because she believed that he who had made the promise would be faithful to it. 12Because of this, there came from one man, and one who was already as good as dead himself, *more descendants than could be counted, as many as the stars of heaven or the grains of sand on the seashore.*[b]

---

11 b. Gn 22:17, also quoted in Ex 32.

¹³All these died in faith, before receiving any of the things that had been promised, but they saw them in the far distance and welcomed them, recognising that they were only *strangers and nomads on earth.* ¹⁴People who use such terms about themselves make it quite plain that they are in search of their real homeland. ¹⁵They can hardly have meant the country they came from, since they had the opportunity to go back to it; ¹⁶but in fact they were longing for a better homeland, their heavenly homeland. That is why God is not ashamed to be called their God, since he has founded the city for them.

¹⁷It was by faith that Abraham, *when put to the test, offered up Isaac.*ᶜ He offered to sacrifice his only son even though the promises had been made to him ¹⁸and he had been told: *It is through Isaac that your name will be carried on.*ᵈ ¹⁹He was confident that God had the power even to raise the dead; and so, figuratively speaking, he was given back Isaac from the dead.

²⁰It was by faith that this same Isaac gave his blessing to Jacob and Esau for the still distant future. ²¹By faith Jacob, when he was dying, blessed each of Joseph's sons, *leaning on the end of his stick as though bowing to pray.*ᵉ ²²It was by faith that, when he was about to die, Joseph recalled the Exodus of the Israelites and made the arrangements for his own burial.

---

11 c. Gn 22:1-14.   11 d. Gn 21:12.   11 e. Gn 47:31.

²³It was by faith that Moses, when he was born, *was hidden by his parents for three months;* they defied the royal edict when they *saw* he was such a *fine* child. ²⁴It was by faith that, *when he grew to manhood,* Moses refused to be known as the son of Pharaoh's daughter ²⁵and chose to be ill-treated in company with God's people rather than to enjoy for a time the pleasures of sin. ²⁶He considered that the insults offered to the Anointed were something more precious than all the treasures of Egypt, because he had his eyes fixed on the reward. ²⁷It was by faith that he left Egypt and was not afraid of the king's anger; he held to his purpose like a man who could see the Invisible. ²⁸It was by faith that he kept *the Passover* and sprinkled *the blood* to prevent *the Destroyer* from touching any of the first-born sons of Israel. ²⁹It was by faith they crossed the Red Sea as easily as dry land, while the Egyptians, trying to do the same, were drowned.

³⁰It was through faith that the walls of Jericho fell down when the people had been round them for seven days. ³¹It was by faith that Rahab the prostitute welcomed the spies and so was not killed with the unbelievers.

³²Is there any need to say more? There is not time for me to give an account of Gideon, Barak, Samson, Jephthah, or of David, Samuel and the prophets. ³³These were men who through faith conquered kingdoms, did what is right and earned the promises. They could keep a

lion's mouth shut, [34]put out blazing fires and emerge unscathed from battle. They were weak people who were given strength, to be brave in war and drive back foreign invaders. [35]Some came back to their wives from the dead, by resurrection; and others submitted to torture, refusing release so that they would rise again to a better life. [36]Some had to bear being pilloried and flogged, or even chained up in prison. [37]They were stoned, or sawn in half,[f] or beheaded; they were homeless, and dressed in the skins of sheep and goats; they were penniless and were given nothing but ill-treatment. [38]They were too good for the world and they went out to live in deserts and mountains and in caves and ravines. [39]These are all heroes of faith, but they did not receive what was promised, [40]since God had made provision for us to have something better, and they were not to reach perfection except with us.

The example of Jesus Christ

12[1]With so many witnesses in a great cloud on every side of us, we too, then, should throw off everything that hinders us, especially the sin that clings so easily, and keep running steadily in the race we have started. [2]Let us not lose sight of Jesus, who leads us in our faith and brings it to perfection: for the sake of the

---

[11 f] Some apocryphal books say that this was how King Manasseh had Isaiah executed.

joy which was still in the future, he endured the cross, disregarding the shamefulness of it, and *from now on has taken his place at the right* of God's throne. ³Think of the way he stood such opposition from sinners and then you will not give up for want of courage. ⁴In the fight against sin, you have not yet had to keep fighting to the point of death.

God's fatherly instruction

⁵Have you forgotten that encouraging text in which you are addressed as sons? *My son, when the Lord corrects you, do not treat it lightly; but do not get discouraged when he reprimands you. ⁶For the Lord trains the ones that he loves and he punishes all those that he acknowledges as his sons.*[a] ⁷Suffering is part of your *training*; God is treating you as his *sons*. Has there ever been any *son* whose father did not *train* him? ⁸If you were not getting this training, as all of you are, then you would not be *sons* but bastards. ⁹Besides, we have all had our human fathers who punished us, and we respected them for it; we ought to be even more willing to submit ourselves to our spiritual Father, to be given life. ¹⁰Our human fathers were thinking of this short life when they punished us, and could only do what they thought best; but he does it all for our own good, so that we may share his own holiness.

---

12 a. Ps 3:11-12 (LXX).

[11]Of course, any punishment is most painful at the time, and far from pleasant; but later, in those on whom it has been used, it bears fruit in peace and goodness. [12]So *hold up your limp arms and steady your trembling knees*[b] [13]and *smooth out the path you tread;*[c] then the injured limb will not be wrenched, it will grow strong again.

Unfaithfulness is punished

[14]*Always be wanting peace*[d] with all people, and the holiness without which no one can ever see the Lord. [15]Be careful that no one is deprived of the grace of God and that no *root of bitterness should begin to grow and make trouble;*[e] this can poison a whole community. [16]And be careful that there is no immorality, or that any of you does not degrade religion like Esau, *who sold his birthright* for one single meal. [17]As you know, when he wanted to obtain the blessing afterwards, he was rejected and, though he pleaded for it with tears, he was unable to elicit a change of heart.

The two covenants

[18]What you have come to is nothing known to the senses: not a *blazing fire,*[f] or a *gloom* turning to *total darkness*, or a *storm;* [19]or *trumpeting thunder* or the

---

[12 b.] Is 35:3. [12 c.] Pr 4:26 (LXX). [12 d.] Ps 34:14. [12 e.] Dt 29:17. [12 f.] The quotations in vv. 18-20 are from Ex 19 (recalled in Dt 4).

great voice speaking which made everyone that heard it beg that no more should be said to them. [20]They were appalled at the order that was given: *If even an animal touches the mountain, it must be stoned.* [21]The whole scene was so terrible that Moses said: *I am afraid,*[g] and was trembling with fright. [22]But what you have come to is Mount Zion and the city of the living God, the heavenly Jerusalem where the millions of angels have gathered for the festival, [23]with the whole Church in which everyone is a 'first-born son' and a citizen of heaven. You have come to God himself, the supreme Judge, and been placed with the spirits of the saints who have been made perfect; [24]and to Jesus, the mediator who brings a new covenant and a blood for purification which pleads more insistently than Abel's. [25]Make sure that you never refuse to listen when he speaks. The people who refused to listen to the warning from a voice on earth could not escape their punishment, and how shall we escape if we turn away from a voice that warns us from heaven? [26]That time his voice made the earth shake, but now he has given us this promise: *I shall make the earth shake once more and* not only the earth but *heaven as well.*[h] [27]The words *once more* show that since the things being shaken are created things, they are going to be

---

[12g.] Dt 9:19.   [12h.] Hg 2:6, probably influenced also by Ps 68:8.

changed, so that the unshakeable things will be left. [28]We have been given possession of an unshakeable kingdom. Let us therefore hold on to the grace that we have been given and use it to worship God in the way that he finds acceptable, in reverence and fear. [29]For our *God* is a *consuming fire*.[i]

APPENDIX

Final recommendations

13 [1]Continue to love each other like brothers, [2]and remember always to welcome strangers, for by doing this, some people have entertained angels without knowing it. [3]Keep in mind those who are in prison, as though you were in prison with them; and those who are being badly treated, since you too are in the one body. [4]Marriage is to be honoured by all, and marriages are to be kept undefiled, because fornicators and adulterers will come under God's judgement. [5]Put greed out of your lives and be content with whatever you have; God himself has said: *I will not fail you or desert you*,[a] [6]and so we can say with confidence: *With the Lord to help me, I fear nothing: what can man do to me?*[b]

[12 i.] Dt 4:24.
[13 a.] Dt 31:6.   [13 b.] Ps 118:6; Ps 27:1.

Faithfulness

⁷Remember your leaders, who preached the word of God to you, and as you reflect on the outcome of their lives, imitate their faith. ⁸Jesus Christ is the same today as he was yesterday and as he will be for ever. ⁹Do not let yourselves be led astray by all sorts of strange doctrines: it is better to rely on grace for inner strength than on dietary laws which have done no good to those who kept them. ¹⁰We have our own altar from which those who serve the tabernacle have no right to eat. ¹¹The bodies of the animals *whose blood is brought into the sanctuary* by the high priest *for the atonement of sin are burnt outside the camp,*ᶜ ¹²and so Jesus too suffered outside the gate to sanctify the people with his own blood. ¹³Let us go to him, then, *outside the camp*, and share his degradation. ¹⁴For there is no eternal city for us in this life but we look for one in the life to come. ¹⁵Through him, *let us offer God* an unending *sacrifice of praise,*ᵈ a verbal sacrifice that is offered every time we acknowledge his name. ¹⁶Keep doing good works and sharing your resources, for these are sacrifices that please God.

Obedience to religious leaders

¹⁷Obey your leaders and do as they tell you, because they must give an account of the way they look after your souls; make this a joy for them to do, and not a grief - you

¹³ᶜ· Lv 16:27.   ¹³ᵈ· Ps 50:14.

yourselves would be the losers. [18]We are sure that our own conscience is clear and we are certainly determined to behave honourably in everything we do; pray for us. [19]I ask you very particularly to pray that I may come back to you all the sooner.

EPILOGUE

News, good wishes and greetings

[20]I pray that the God of peace, *who brought* our Lord Jesus *back*[e] from the dead *to become the great Shepherd of the sheep*[f] *by the blood that sealed an eternal covenant,*[g] [21]may make you ready to do his will in any kind of good action; and turn us all into whatever is acceptable to himself through Jesus Christ, to whom be glory for ever and ever, Amen.

[22]I do ask you, brothers, to take these words of advice kindly; that is why I have written to you so briefly.

[23]I want you to know that our brother Timothy has been set free. If he arrives in time, he will be with me when I see you. [24]Greetings to all your leaders and to all the saints. The saints of Italy send you greetings. [25]Grace be with you all.

---

13 e. Is 63:11.   13 f. Ezk 34:23.   13 g. Ezk 37:26.

Compendium of the

CATECHISM OF THE
CATHOLIC CHURCH

"The *Compendium*, which I now present to the Universal Church, is a faithful and sure synthesis of the *Catechism of the Catholic Church*. It contains, in concise form, all the essential and fundamental elements of the Church's faith, thus constituting, as my Predecessor had wished, a kind of *vademecum*, which allows believers and non-believers alike to behold the entire panorama of the Catholic faith.".

Benedictus PP XVI

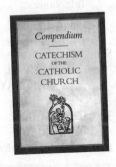

Compendium
CATECHISM
OF THE
CATHOLIC
CHURCH

ISBN 1 86082 376 9
CTS Code: Do 742

Informative Catholic Reading

We hope that you have enjoyed reading this booklet.

If you would like to find out more about CTS booklets - we'll send you our free information pack and catalogue.

Please send us your details:

Name ....

Address ....

....

....

Postcode ....

Telephone ....

Email ....

Send to: CTS, 40-46 Harleyford Road,
            Vauxhall, London
            SE11 5AY

Tel: 020 7640 0042
Fax: 020 7640 0046
Email: info@cts-online.org.uk